Perfectly Balanced

GOLF

YOUR KEY TO A WINNING GAME

FOREWORDS BY

Tom Kite, Payne Stewart, and Corey Pavin

U.S. Open Champions

Chuck Cook

with Roger Schiffman

DOUBLEDAY

New York   London   Toronto   Sydney   Auckland

PUBLISHED BY DOUBLEDAY
a division of Bantam Doubleday Dell Publishing Group, Inc.
1540 Broadway, New York, New York 10036

DOUBLEDAY and the portrayal of an anchor with a dolphin are trademarks of
Doubleday, a division of Bantam Doubleday Dell Publishing Group, Inc.

Book design by Richard Oriolo

Instruction photographs by Stephen Szurlej

Library of Congress Cataloging-in-Publication Data

Cook, Chuck.
Perfectly balanced golf : your key to a winning game / Chuck Cook with Roger Schiffman :
foreWords by Tom Kite, Payne Steward, and Corey Pavin. — 1st ed.
p.   cm.
1. Golf.   I. Schiffman, Roger, 1955–   . II. Title.
GV965.C662   1997
796.352—dc21   97-28932
CIP

ISBN 0-385-48670-7

Printed in the United States of America

November 1997

First Edition

1   3   5   7   9   10   8   6   4   2

This book is dedicated to Greg and Katie.
C.C.

For Patty and Kate.
R.S.

CONTENTS

F O R E W O R D
by Tom Kite

When I was a kid growing up in Texas, my first teacher was Harvey Penick. He gave me an understanding of golf that has allowed me to improve for most of my career. But when I went on the PGA Tour in 1973, I found I needed to make some adjustments in my swing. This was to better handle the different types of courses and weather conditions I encountered. It was about this time that I first met Chuck Cook, and by the mid-1980s I was working with him almost full-time. Therefore, it gives me great pleasure to write this foreword for *Perfectly Balanced Golf*.

Chuck has long been one of the most inquisitive of the better teachers. He has talked to most of the top players and probably all of the top teachers in the game. This has given him a true understanding of cause and effect in the golf swing. I recall once when I was getting some help from Mr. Penick, Chuck just happened to be around watching the lessons. When Mr. Penick had finished making his suggestions, Chuck approached him and asked how he knew exactly what to suggest. Mr. Penick told him that when he had been Chuck's age, he was not as sure either. It takes years to become one of the best teachers, just as it takes years to become one of the top players. Chuck has now done his homework.

There can be no better example of this than the fact that Chuck has worked with three recent U.S. Open champions: Corey Pavin, Payne Stewart, and myself. The interesting thing is that although the wins are similar, the styles and swings are about as different as they can be. Right now, with all the "method" teachers around, how can one teacher work with three so vastly different players and have success? The secret lies in the fact that Chuck truly understands cause and effect. Chuck is not a stickler for making every swing look alike. He is a stickler for the fact that if a student wants to hit a certain type of shot, then certain things must happen. This is why Corey, Payne, and I all feel so comfortable working with Chuck. He only helps us do what we want to do.

What does this mean to the average golfer? It means that Chuck can work with the students' natural abilities to help produce the optimum performance. Too often, golfers come away from their lessons more confused and frustrated than they were before the instruction. This does not happen with Chuck in control. He does not overteach; he simplifies. He does not demand; he suggests changes. He gets results. His students all improve! Pay close attention to *Perfectly Balanced Golf* and you have to improve, too.

Anyone who has ever picked up a club and attempted to strike a golf ball has an appreciation for the complexity of the activity. The relative importance of greater strength or stature seen in most athletic competition is replaced by the more critical need for timing and control. Nevertheless, mastering the mechanical aspects of the game is only the beginning of competitive golf. The highest level of play, as in any art form, is a blending of the "science" of the game with the uniquely personal contribution of the golfer.

Being committed to the melding of the uniquely personal with the technical is the hallmark of a great golf coach. It is this quality that makes Chuck Cook one of the best coaches in professional golf today. Not content with simply forcing his players into one specific style, he takes each person as an individual with an eye to capitalizing on his or her strengths. This principle of his instruction is perhaps best illustrated by considering the three U.S. Open champions with whom he has worked. Each of us employs a decidedly different swing. Rather than have us change and conform to some elusive ideal, Chuck recognizes the artistry in our individual techniques and works to develop it.

My association with Chuck has been both professional and personal. When you work with someone for as long as I have with Chuck, it is hard to distinguish between the lessons concerning golf and the more general lessons about life. Together we have shared a lot of golf and life. I would not trade the times we have shared on and off the golf course for anything in the world.

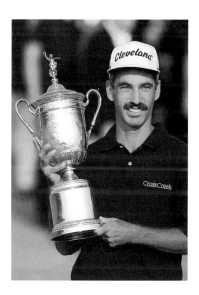

I started working with Chuck Cook during the 1995 Tournament Players Championship. I knew that both Tom Kite and Payne Stewart had won U.S. Opens while working with Chuck, and I wanted to raise my game another notch, too. At that time, I was considered the "best player to never have won a major," and while that label didn't bother me, I knew I was capable of winning a major championship.

Chuck worked with me on developing a draw for more distance. I could always maneuver the ball both ways, but I was never as comfortable drawing the ball. I now use a drill in which I close my stance, aiming 40 yards to the right of where I want the ball to finish, and hit against my left side. In this way, Chuck helped me "balance out," so to speak, my ball flight.

In the first fourteen months I worked with Chuck, I won three tournaments—one was the U.S. Open and one had a million-dollar first prize. My PGA Tour statistics improved dramatically in both distance and accuracy: I rose twenty-six spots in hitting greens in regulation, and I gained an average 6 yards in driving distance. Both were very positive improvements.

You probably saw the 4-wood shot I hit to the 72nd green at Shinnecock Hills to clinch the 1995 U.S. Open. And you probably noticed that the shot turned from right to left. That shot was a result of confidence. Chuck and I had done a lot of work earlier that week and in the weeks leading up to the Open. I was simply on my game at Shinnecock, able to hit the shots that were called for—high, low, left-to-right, and right-to-left. My game was in perfect balance. Under pressure, I had the confidence to hit that 4-wood shot. It was a tremendous feeling.

Needless to say, I think Chuck Cook is an excellent teacher. To me, the single most important attribute of a great teacher, after he has acquired a sound knowledge of the swing, is the ability to communicate. Chuck can express his thoughts in ten different ways. Every student needs to be taught in a personal style, and Chuck has that unique capability.

Chuck Cook helped me raise my game to a new level, and I'm sure he can do the same for you.

The History Behind

This Book

Pretty is as pretty does.
—HARVEY PENICK

This book is designed to give you a method for developing your game to its maximum level. This might involve winning the fourth flight of your club championship, or perhaps winning the U.S. Open, as Tom Kite, Payne Stewart, and Corey Pavin have done using the principles I am going to present.

You'll notice I said develop *your* game. You might also know that Tom Kite, Payne Stewart, and Corey Pavin have very different methods. You see, there is no best way for everyone to play golf, but there is a best way for *you* to play golf. Tom, Payne, and Corey have found *their* best ways, and my goal in this book is to help you find *your* best way.

I came to the conclusion that there is not one best method for playing

golf after I traveled along a winding but typical journey for a developing teacher. I began my teaching career as an assistant professional in Indiana, where most of my instruction consisted of telling students what *I* did with the golf club. I guess you could call this the "Chuck Cook Method." I found that I helped some people, hurt some, and left a lot the same. When I decided to specialize as a teacher of golf, rather than be a general club professional, I went to work as an instructor in the Golf Digest Schools. I had an enviable opportunity to apprentice under such famous teachers as Bob Toski, Jim Flick, Davis Love, Jr., Peter Kostis, Paul Runyan, John Jacobs, and many others. This was my first exposure to the methods of others. I now could teach someone using not only the "Chuck Cook Method" but also the "Bob Toski Method," the "Jim Flick Method," the . . . well, you get the picture. This was a real awakening to the fact that not only do players swing differently with equal success, but teachers teach differently with equal success. I was also becoming vaguely aware that some "methods" fit certain types of players better than others.

I can remember kneeling down and teeing balls for these great teachers. I would try to guess what they were going to say to the student. Then I'd listen and see how close I came to thinking the way they did. Jim Flick, Peter Kostis, and John Jacobs were reasonably predictable. Bob Toski and the late Davis Love, Jr., always stumped me.

After spending a number of years in the Golf Digest program, I was hired to start the Academy of Golf in Austin, Texas. This was a beautifully designed facility that encompassed a state-of-the-art driving range, several short-game areas, a clubhouse, a covered teaching shelter, and, most unusually, three actual golf holes—a par 3, a par 4, and a par 5. This being the first facility of its kind, I wanted to create programs that would match the stature of the physical plant itself. Therefore, I hired an advisory board whose purpose was to develop procedures based on *fact* rather than on opinion. This group was composed of Dr. Ralph Mann (a former Olympic hurdler and presently biomechanics engineer), Dr. Richard Coop (an educational psychologist), Al Vermeil (a physiologist who is currently the strength coach of the Chicago Bulls), and Dave Pelz (a noted researcher in the short-game and golf-equipment fields). We conducted golf schools using the skills of each of the advisors. In addition, we gathered research to find out how people actually play the game.

This group generated a lot of "heady" information for a golf teacher to try to use and disseminate. To help in this area, I also hired Jack Nicklaus's personal instructor at that time, Phil Rodgers. Phil, although somewhat of an iconoclast, contributed many novel ideas that we tried at the Academy, thereby developing the "Academy Method." I was still caught up in trying to teach everyone the same information and in the same manner.

At the time, I was also speaking at a number of PGA of America teaching workshops, where I had the opportunity to present these ideas next to such eminent instructors as Dr. Gary Wiren, Derek Hardy, Bill Strausbaugh, David Leadbetter, and Ed Oldfield, to name a few.

Then, five things happened that broke me of the "method" mentality. First, I met and listened to the aforementioned Ed Oldfield. He had a method, but it was diametrically opposed to what Phil Rodgers and I were teaching. Ed was famous at that time for creating superstars on the LPGA Tour, having nurtured such top players as Jan Stephenson, Betsy King, and Alice Miller. In the schools Phil and I were doing, I noticed that women had a particularly hard time adapting to our system. So I began trying some of Ed's principles with women and had instant success.

Second, I had the opportunity to watch Ben Hogan hit practice balls at Shady Oaks. At the time, Phil and I were teaching an upright swing (à la Nicklaus) with a lot of hand action that produced very little divot and a high ball flight. Hogan swung on a much flatter plane, "drove" the ball more (thereby creating an obvious divot), and hit it considerably lower than the way we were teaching.

Third, in hiring Dick Coop to help me with the psychology of teaching and playing golf, I was presented with the knowledge that not only do people swing differently, but, more important, they think differently, again with equal success. What Dick made me realize was that all people are equally "smart." It's how they use their "smarts" that varies. Some people use them in an intellectual or analytical fashion. You might call them "book smart." Others use their thinking in a more intuitive, feel-oriented manner. You might call them "street smart." Since there was certainly a lot of evidence that neither way was superior, I realized I had to stop teaching a method. I'll discuss this in more detail as we go along, but I can assure you that without

"All teachers teach differently."
—HARVEY PENICK

Dick Coop's tutelage, I would never have developed the ability to help such diverse players as Tom Kite and Payne Stewart.

Fourth, I became interested in *The Golfing Machine* by Homer Kelley. This book talks about the laws of physics and geometry as related to the golf swing and lists hundreds of possible *variations* players can use to play golf successfully. While I am still an undergraduate in learning all of the things this exceptional work has to offer, my guides—Ben Doyle, Tom Ness, and Mac O'Grady—have been quite patient in helping me help others. These talented teachers are well versed in Kelley's writings and have been more than happy to share their knowledge with me.

Finally, I met the late Harvey Penick. Of all the people I've met in golf, there is no one in the same category with Harvey. (He insisted on being called Harvey. "Mr. Penick was my dad," he would always say.) Harvey was an absolute genius at teaching golf *and* life. From the time I started living in Austin, I took as many opportunities as I could to watch Harvey teach, and I've vicariously learned more about his teaching by reliving lessons he gave to people I've met in Austin. (Most of the people who have lived there and played much golf have one or several "Harvey stories.") He showed me how much more important it is for a student to refine his or her *natural* ability than to retool into a method that might be contrary to his or her instincts. Harvey taught and coached four members of the LPGA Hall of Fame (Kathy Whitworth, Mickey Wright, Betsy Rawls, and Betty Jameson), as well as numerous PGA Tour players, Tom Kite and Ben Crenshaw being the most notable. If you look at all of these great champions, the most obvious feature is that they all swing differently. And all of them have swings that match their natural manner. Notice the near-perfect but constructed form of Mickey Wright and Tom Kite, or the natural freedom of Kathy Whitworth and Ben Crenshaw. Harvey once said, "A real trouble with a lot of players is that they try to develop somebody else's style instead of their own. I want a player to develop a sound golf swing. I don't want the 'look good' part of it overdone. If they're sound, they usually look good enough." The players mentioned above are all *different* and *successful.*

That's what I'd like to help you do—be successful with your golf game. To do that, we need to find *your* best way to play golf. Now let's look at how I'd like you to use this book.

How to Use

This Book

Your golf game is working when it produces shots that go to the target on a reasonably consistent basis. To do that, of course, a golf swing must have certain elements that produce controlled direction, distance, trajectory, and consistency. However, those elements aren't the same for all players. For instance, Lee Trevino developed a golf swing that aimed left, had a grip that would generally produce shots going to the left, and had a swing path generally attributed to people who spin the ball to the left; but he consistently hit shots that went to the right! On the opposite side of the scale, Arnold Palmer aimed to the right, had a grip that would generally produce shots going to the right, and hit shots that worked to the left!

LEE TREVINO
AIMS LEFT AND
PUSHES THE
BALL TOWARD
THE TARGET . . .

. . . WHILE
ARNOLD PALMER
AIMS RIGHT AND
PULL-HOOKS THE
BALL BACK TO
THE TARGET.

How does this happen, and how can you use such information? The key is to develop a *compatible* arrangement of components, one that produces a balanced golf swing, which in turn produces a usable shot. An unbalanced arrangement of those components will produce an unusable shot.

But to counterbalance the various parts of your swing into a balanced whole, you must have a center from which to measure. Chapter 4 offers this centered golf game. I'm not suggesting it as a model but, rather, as a base from which you can work. You can see why this is necessary. If one of your counterbalance corrections involves turning your hands more to the right on your grip, for example, you need to know "more to the right of what?" The "what" in this instance would be the centered grip described in Chapter 4.

So I'd like to see you read Chapter 4 first, then use the remaining chapters to design your own golf game. For instance, if you want to alter your game to hit the ball lower, you will then go to Chapter 7 and use one or more of the principles described there. If you want to change the curvature of your ball flight and make a draw your bread-and-butter shot, you will turn to Chapter 5 and use one or more of the principles described there, and so on.

Within Chapter 4, I've provided an easy reference guide in chart form so you can look up any shot tendency and quickly find the appropriate counterbalances (see page 41). Studying this chart on its own will give you an overview of cause and effect in the golf swing. I recommend using it as a refresher course anytime your swing goes awry.

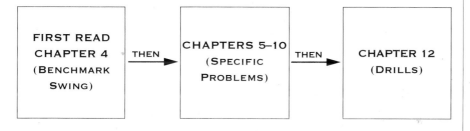

TO GET THE MOST BENEFIT FROM THIS BOOK, I RECOMMEND YOU READ IT IN THIS MANNER.

Chapter 12 is a chapter of drills. Every drill that is prescribed or suggested in the other chapters is covered in detail in Chapter 12. This is the part of the book that will actually be most valuable to your quick progression as a student. Performing a drill, even for just a few minutes every day, is the surest and fastest way to change a component in your swing. Why? Because the drill isolates the problem and provides a specific correction. So take note when a drill is offered in a section of the book that pertains to your problem or to your goal. Find the drill in Chapter 12 and rehearse it. You'll be amazed how easy it is to alter your swing or your shot patterns with these drills.

Frankly, this is what most successful players do when developing their style of play. I hope this book helps you to enjoy this great game more—and maybe someday *you* will win the U.S. Open!

"Major surgery requires major recovery time."
—HARVEY PENICK

A final note: You'll find an unusual feature in this book. At any point where I think it appropriate, I'll include a quote from the teacher who most influenced me and my teaching—Harvey Penick. While each quote might relate to other points on the page, just skimming through the Penick quotes should be a worthwhile endeavor regardless of their context.

So let's get started!

Balancing Your Game

on the Golf Course

Mickey Wright once told Harvey Penick, the legendary teacher from Austin, Texas, that she wished she could get her hands high at the top of the swing like Betsy Rawls. "You really don't want your hands high like Betsy," Harvey said. "You just like what she has done with her hands high!" In other words, Harvey wanted Mickey to play her own game, to develop her own style, to find her own balance. And that's what I will try to help you do.

Most golf books start out with the grip and then go to the stance and then to posture and alignment and then to the swing itself. They tell you that this is the way you ought to play golf. This book is different. My contention: How can you know what grip to use, what posture, what type of alignment, what kinds of clubs, before you know what kind of golfer you want to be or can be? No two people—and no two golfers—are the same. We all have different strengths and weaknesses. Before we can decide what kind of swing we should use, and what style of golf we should play, we must consider three areas:

1. Your physical characteristics. Your body makeup determines what you can and cannot do.

2. Your environmental makeup. Where do you play geographically, what kind of grasses do you play on, and what is the general terrain of the courses in your area?

3. Third, your mental makeup. How does your mind work when you're playing golf and when you're participating in other activities?

Your Physical Characteristics

To play golf well, either you must be strong or you must be flexible. There are golf swings designed around people who are strong and around people who are flexible. Consequently, you need to be one or the other, or, ideally, both.

If you are strong but not flexible, then you should use what I call a *hitting* style of play. Golfers in this group would include thick-chested, heavy-set men who have strong arms and wrists—people who might do a lot of physical work. Also, many senior golfers lose their flexibility before they lose their strength and might do well to adopt a hitting style. These players use leverage rather than centrifugal force to propel the ball (in Chapter 4, see the sections "The Balanced Movement of the Club" and "The Balanced Movement of the Body").

If you are flexible but not strong, you should use a *swinging* style rather than a hitting style. This group would include a lot of women. Often they are not as strong as men, and their style of play should be developed around their greater flexibility.

If you are both strong and flexible, like many of today's Tour players, then you'll have an option to play either as a hitter or as a swinger. In general, hitting is more versatile, whereas swinging is more consistent.

"I'd like to see women play with longer clubs, not shorter clubs."
—HARVEY PENICK

PERFECTLY BALANCED GOLF

I can remember when the different styles of play came to me. I was watching Dan Pohl on the driving range at a Tour event in California. He was one of the Tour's longest hitters but had a backswing length that could be called three-quarters at best, but a longer-than-average follow-through. I asked him how he hit it so far, and he told me he just "cocked it and whopped it. It's like driving a nail with a hammer."

So, the first thing you have to decide about yourself: Are you strong or flexible, or are you both? If you are neither, then I would recommend you start an exercise program based on a book like the one produced by the Centinela Hospital (in Los Angeles), which lists some thirty exercises for improving your golf-related muscles in terms of strength and flexibility.

Players on the Tour who are strong but not especially flexible are Craig Stadler and Ed Fiori. Dottie Pepper, on the women's Tour, is a good example of a successful player who is very flexible but not especially strong. The players who are both are the better athletes—Tiger Woods, Greg Norman, Tom Watson, Ernie Els.

Your Environmental Makeup

If Jack Nicklaus, with his upright golf swing, had grown up in west Texas, where the fairways are firm and the wind blows really hard, and where it's better to hit the ball down and let it run rather than hit high, floating shots, then you might never have heard of him. By the same token, if Lee Trevino, with his type of low ball flight, had played all of his golf at Scioto, where Nicklaus played, or at Augusta National, then you probably would never have heard of him either.

So the first thing you have to look at is the course or courses you play most regularly. Determine if the fairways are hard and fast, or slow. If they are fast, then you will probably want to hit the ball lower so it will roll farther. If the fairways are soft, you might want to hit the ball high, to get maximum carry.

Then determine the characteristics of your greens. Are there any elevation changes? If there are a lot of greens on top of hills, or mounds in the fairways that you have to carry from the tees, then you will need to hit the ball high. If you're playing where there is not a lot of variation in the elevation, then you will need to hit the ball low. Florida and Texas are perfect examples of where it's best to hit the ball low. Playing in New York's Westchester County or in parts of New England requires a high ball flight. Another area that allows you to hit the ball high is San Diego, California. The weather there is perfect most of the year: lots of sun, not much wind.

ARE THE COURSES YOU PLAY GENERALLY FLAT, WITH LITTLE ELEVATION TO THE PUTTING SURFACES . . .

. . . OR ARE THEY HILLY, REQUIRING HIGH APPROACHES TO THE GREENS?

I taught with Phil Rodgers for a while, and he is from San Diego. He was adamant about hitting high shots from both long range and around the green. His style of teaching encouraged a very sweeping blow with the club to produce these high shots. When he went back to play on the Senior Tour, where a lot of tournaments are played in windy Florida, he had to retool.

Next, you have to figure out what shape of shot best suits the golf course. Augusta National, for example, requires that a lot of shots be hit with a draw. Colonial Country Club in Fort Worth is just the opposite. There you have a lot of doglegs to the right. Ben Hogan was so successful there because he played a fade. Where is the predominance of trouble, on the left or the right? If you play one course most of the time, then you want a game that suits that course.

Next, ask yourself at what level you play. For instance, at the Tour level, where you play all sorts of different courses all over the country, to be successful you need a fairly neutral golf swing. You can't be a player who hits a big, sweeping hook or a big slice, or who can only hit the ball high or only hit it low. You're going to run into too many situations where your game won't be applicable. Consequently, as you look through this book, if you have Tour aspirations you want to be as closely in balance as you can get. If you play regionally, then you may need a specific type of ball flight to be successful in your area.

Finally, look at your lifestyle. How much time have you got to practice? If you don't have much time to spend on the range, then you have to take your normal ball flight and work on strategies that allow the best use of that flight.

Your Mental Makeup

Look at whether you are an aggressive or a conservative player. To be an aggressive player, the one thing you need is enough distance. If you are a short hitter, the fastest way to improve might be to change to a more aggressive style. If you are a long hitter, you might have to adopt a more conservative style.

If you are an emotional player, you may need to tighten the reins a bit. Colin Montgomerie is a good example of a Tour player who improved when he became less demonstrative and more in control. Tom Kite is an example of the opposite. He became a great player when he became more emotional on the course—taking more chances—and less controlled. Your golf game needs to be such that it will blend with your emotional makeup.

Also, determine whether you are an analytical or an intuitive type of player. An analytical player is very good at the preswing things—strategy, setup and aim, ball position, attention to such details as the lie, assessment of the wind, and so forth. Ben Hogan, Nick Faldo, and Tom Kite are good examples. An analytical player probably needs to develop more touch and feel, things that are not his or her strong suit—in-between shots, swinging more gracefully.

An intuitive player, like a Payne Stewart or a Ben Crenshaw or a Sam Snead, needs to work on analytical things, like proper yardages and alignment. Again, what we're looking for is a way to balance out certain characteristics.

This book is designed to help you do that.

"I wouldn't let Tommy [Kite] watch Ben [Crenshaw] take a lesson or Ben watch Tommy."
—HARVEY PENICK

The Balance Beam
for Your Golf Game

The purpose of this chapter is to give you a benchmark from which you can spin your own personal preferences to design *your* golf game. It's like a balance beam in gymnastics. To stay on the beam, you must be in perfect balance. But if you waver to one side, you must counterbalance yourself to keep from falling. In most books on how to play golf, the author will start with the setup, go on to the backswing, then (yawn) the downswing, impact, and finish. What I'll present here, however, will be the order in which you must make the decisions that will determine *your* style of play. All shots begin in the *mind*, so I'll discuss the mental game first. You then have to decide how the *ball* must get to the target, so I'll cover the ball's flight next. To make the ball go to the target, the *club* has to strike it, so we'll discuss the club action needed to produce the chosen ball flight. Finally, the *body* must move the club that strikes the ball toward the chosen target, so this chapter will end with a discussion of how the body moves; or rather, this chapter will end where most other how-to golf books start.

THE BALANCED MENTAL GAME

Obviously, the mental game means how you use your brain. Therefore, to fully understand this section, let's look first at a rudimentary explanation of how the brain works. The information presented here was explained to me by Dr. Dick Coop, whom I introduced in Chapter 1.

Feel Versus Analysis

The brain has two sides, with each having different uses. The left side is used for analytical functions, while the right side is used, for the lack of a better term, for feel.

Each of us has both sides, but because of the way we train our minds, we tend to use one side more often than the other. Let's discuss each side in a little more detail and then talk about how its use—and how you use *your* mind—will influence your golf.

Left Brain

The left side of the brain deals with the functions of analysis, verbal ability, computation, logic, sequential planning, and rational thought. Its use in golf would include the analysis of playing conditions such as wind, lie of the ball, temperature, yardage, and so forth; the step-by-step process of the preswing routine; club selection and hole strategy decisions, and other non-movement functions such as alignment. As you can tell, all of these functions are terribly important for good golf.

As mentioned above, because of our training we tend to favor one side of the brain over the other. The training of our left brain takes in most kinds of formal education: mathematics, science, language (conjugation of verbs, etc.), history (the sequence and timing of events), even the arts (learning different drawing techniques, as well as musical notation and formal dance steps). All of these functions form a structure within which we tend to operate. There seems to be a "right" and "wrong" way of doing things in most formal education. Therefore, those of you with higher degrees might tend to be overbalanced toward the left side of your brain.

The constant use of the left brain in your daily life will tend to shape your personality in golf as in most other things. Thus, if you're an engineer, an accountant, a lawyer, or a computer programmer, on the golf course you will probably be known as an analytical player, a "smart" player, or even a mechanical player.

Golfers on the PGA Tour who come to mind when describing this mode: Tom Kite, Nick Faldo, Mark O'Meara, and (from the past) Ben Hogan. These are players who use a very formal, structured swing and golf technique, and who are known to have mechanically sound methods. They rarely make mental mistakes, generally are quite consistent, and love to practice their techniques.

BEN HOGAN HAS BECOME NEARLY SYNONYMOUS WITH THE TERM "ANALYTICAL." HE WOULD BE CONSIDERED A "LEFT-BRAIN" PLAYER.

If you feel you lean toward this category, based on this description, be aware of the strengths you have.

Right Brain

The right side of the brain deals with the functions of intuition, creativity, imagination, orientation in space, and emotions and feelings. Its use in golf would include visualization of ball flight and roll; estimation of distance on in-between shots; feel; tempo; and imagination on trouble shots. Again, very important ingredients for good golf.

The training of the right brain involves activities like reaction sports, music, free-style art, acting, and so forth. This right side of the brain doesn't feel much structure and may not have much of a black-and-white view of things. In fact, many right-brainers rebel against structure.

Again, the constant use of the right brain will influence your personality in golf and in life. You may be into sales, advertising, marketing, entre-

preneurship, public entertainment, raising children, or sports. And in golf, you may be known as a "natural" player, an unorthodox player, or a graceful player.

Golfers who are predominant in this mode: Payne Stewart, Seve Ballesteros, Ben Crenshaw, Arnold Palmer, and (from the past) Sam Snead. These are players who play a lot of different shots, who are prone to streaks of brilliant play as well as periodic slumps, and who don't worry about the "right" way or "wrong" way of doing things.

If you feel you tend toward this way of thinking, note the strengths you possess.

The Balanced Use of Your Mind

One of the most important things I've learned in life is that all people are equally "smart." It's merely how we use our minds that makes us different. For instance, you can see the pluses and minuses of being too dependent on the use of one side of the brain over the other: the overly analytical type who is considered brilliant by IQ standards (the tests being based on formal education) but is quite clumsy when trying to do anything athletic; or the athlete who hasn't had much formal education but has great dexterity. We all have available the use of both sides of our brains. To be the most balanced, we should know how to use each side in the way it has been designed.

Golfers able to do this have generally been the dominant players. Harry Vardon, for example, in the earlier years of championship golf, seemed to combine both sides quite well. This placed him a notch above James Braid and J. H. Taylor, the other members of the "Great Triumvirate." Bobby Jones, a little later, was able to dominate Walter Hagen, Gene Sarazen, and Paul Runyan. Byron Nelson was the balanced player between Sam Snead and Ben Hogan. Jack Nicklaus was perhaps the golfer who best combined the skills of analysis and feel. Since then, only Tom Watson and most recently Tiger Woods have given the impression of being balanced. All of those just mentioned have been great champions in their respective eras.

A balanced person uses the analytical side of his or her mind before the swing begins and then switches to the feel, or reactive, side once the swing is in motion. Just picture Jack Nicklaus planning his strategy, picking out his intermediate target as part of a very precise preswing routine, then letting go in the beautiful, free-flowing movement of his swing as he "reaches for the sky" on the backswing.

The more balanced a player becomes, the greater success he has. In 1993, when Tom Kite was shooting 35 under par to win the Bob Hope/Chrysler Desert Classic, he made the comment that he "didn't know what was happening but he was going to ride with it!" This was a definite sign that he had let go of control and was using his right brain more. It was no coincidence that his sport psychologist, Dr. Bob Rotella, was with him that week. Payne Stewart was always a physically talented golfer who had a hard time winning because his lack of structure would catch up with him at crunch time. Dr. Dick Coop worked with Stewart and gave him a preswing routine that stabilized his talent and allowed him to win both the PGA Championship and the U.S. Open.

I will be giving you methods of balancing the mind in a later chapter, but it's important here to have a picture of a balanced golfer.

JACK NICKLAUS, REGARDED BY MANY AS THE BEST TO EVER SWING A GOLF CLUB, WOULD BE CONSIDERED A BALANCED PLAYER.

Aggressive Versus Conservative

In addition to the way in which people *think,* most have a style in which they *react.* To simplify a bit, some of you are aggressive and some of you are conservative. While this reactive style has some parallels to left- and right-brain thinking, it is really a separate consideration.

Aggressive players, obviously, are those who tend to lean toward high-risk decisions, while conservative players tend to lean toward low-risk ones. Generally, high risk leads to greater rewards and greater failures, while low risk leads to lesser rewards and lesser failures.

For instance, when faced with a shot to a pin that is tucked in the right corner of a peninsula green that has water in front, to the right, and behind the pin, an overly aggressive person might shoot at it with no concern for the hazard. If this player pulls it off, he might get the ball close enough to one-putt. If not, he might hit it in the water and run up his score in a hurry. The overly conservative player would never shoot at that pin, always playing to the left of the hole, making the possibility of a one-putt remote but making the probability of hitting in the water just as remote. The player who is balanced in style might shoot at the pin with a wedge but not with a long iron.

If you are an aggressive player, you probably post a lot of high and low scores during a round of golf to come up with your average, whereas if you are a conservative player, you might shoot the same score without the highs and lows but, rather, with a more average score for each hole.

While by nature you may be either aggressive or conservative, you will have to make adjustments to be the best golfer you can be. If you are a smart golfer, you will realize that your style of play is really determined by one variable—the *distance* you hit the ball. Let me explain.

First, let's say you are a 90-percent effective golfer—that is, you miss your target by an average of 10 percent. That means if you have a 100-yard shot, on average you'll miss your target by 10 yards. If you make the *exact same error* from 200 yards, you'll miss your target by 20 yards. Therefore, if you are a short hitter, you have to allow for more room to play to the target because you'll be shooting from a longer distance away.

Second, when a ball is struck by a club, it takes on a spin that is a combination of backspin and sidespin. Obviously, sidespin makes the ball curve more off-line. The more loft a club has, the more backspin (consequently, the less sidespin) the ball takes on. Therefore, it goes straighter. So if you have a longer distance to your target, you have to hit a club that by design will go more crooked! Therefore, a short hitter has to play to avoid disaster much more often than he can play the spectacular shot.

The long hitter, on the other hand, will be able to use shorter clubs with more loft into the greens; therefore, he can play more aggressively because he is using the tools designed to make the ball go straighter. The long hitter, however, has his own set of problems. He has to be more accurate than the short hitter. For instance, take a drive that is

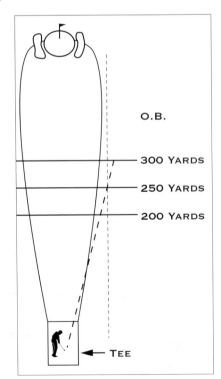

WHY HITTING THE BALL LONGER IS NOT NECESSARILY BETTER.

O.B.

300 YARDS

250 YARDS

200 YARDS

TEE

hit 200 yards but is off-line enough to land barely in the right side of the fairway. An extension of that shot to 250 or 300 yards on the same line might be out of bounds. Therefore, the long hitter must sometimes use his length advantage by backing down to a more-lofted club to stay in play, and then use his distance advantage on the next shot.

Later on, in the section on balancing your mental game, I will give you a method for determining when to be aggressive and when to be conservative. But it's important to understand the pluses and minuses as well as the detriments of your style of play.

The Balanced Mental Round of Golf

For this exercise, we have to ignore the physical aspects of golf, since we are dealing with just the mental side. We are taking a fantasy flight with a player of consummate physical ability and looking at how he would use his mind to play golf. There have been few, if any, players who could or would leave absolutely nothing to chance. In fact, Ben Hogan is the only one I know of. Anyway, we are looking at where we *want* to go, so let's give it a try.

The balanced golfer uses his analytical (left brain) skills long before the round starts by playing practice rounds and developing a *strategy* for playing the course. He then practices the shots most required for that particular venue. For instance, if he were playing Augusta National, he would practice hitting shots high and with a right-to-left shape, since that is what Augusta demands. He might also practice his lag putting, since the course has very large greens and he'll be faced with a lot of longish putts. For example, during the 1980s Tom Kite had a good run of finishes at the Masters. He really prepared a lot. Not only did he work on shaping long shots, but I remember one day we worked on spinning bunker shots in different directions to hold the severe slopes on those greens! If the balanced golfer were playing in Florida or Texas, he might work on hitting lower shots to allow for the wind that is so common there. In fact, I tried to trick Tom Kite a little bit when he was preparing for Florida. I always told him he had the ball too far forward and he'd move it back behind his normal neutral position. During his career, he has won every Florida tournament! When he would come home to prepare for Augusta, I would always tell him he had overdone his ball position and make him move it back up to neutral! If the balanced golfer were playing in the Bob Hope/Chrysler Desert Classic in Palm Springs, California, he might practice his short irons, since the courses used for that tournament are generally short.

Once he arrives at the course, our imaginary player has a particular routine that actually warms up his mind as well as his body. He doesn't use his warm-up time for practice. Practice is done well in advance of the round and after the round. Warm-up is done right before the round.

He'll start off by putting on the practice green, because putting after hitting full shots will only tend to stiffen him up. When putting, he mainly tries to get a feel for the speed of the greens. After doing that, he'll hit a few chips and pitches, and then hit a few bunker shots to become familiar with the texture of the sand. In all of the short shots, he picks particular situations he'll likely encounter while playing—high rough around the green, pot bunkers, long chip shots—all of which he might not encounter in his normal round of golf on another course. He's warming up his mind so that he'll be prepared when he gets on the course. He then starts to hit full shots.

As he begins his full-swing warm-up, he will first warm up his body by hitting shots using a sand wedge. The sand wedge is the heaviest club in the bag, so it serves as a weighted "bat" to loosen up the muscles. This shouldn't take but a few shots. Then he starts hitting with other clubs. During the warm-up, he's not really interested in his swing, only his shots. For instance, if he finds he can only fade the ball while warming up, he'll just allow for it on the course and not try to fix it before playing. Generally, he'll hit a few balls with every *other* club in his bag—pitching wedge, 8-iron, 6 iron, 4 iron, 2-iron, 5-wood, 3-wood, driver. While warming up with those clubs, he'll try to think of particular situations where he might use those clubs and imagine playing them on the course. Before each shot, he might change targets and go through his preswing routine. After working his way through the bag, he will end by practicing his opening tee shot until he has successfully done it a couple of times. He should then be in the best frame of mind to start his round. He has warmed up his "mind" by making his practice "course-specific." He has gotten into his round on the practice field.

Now the round begins. His preround preparation has consisted of selecting the best targets to play to on each hole. This plan should be, in his mind, the *best* way to play the hole, so there should be no reason to change his mind during the round, because any change would mean playing the hole in *less than the best* way.

As he stands on the tee knowing where his target is, he has a couple of decisions to make. The first is where to tee the ball. His rule of thumb in deciding this is to locate the hole's greatest trouble and then tee up on that side. This allows him to aim *away* from trouble.

The second decision involves what kind of shot he wants to play. On a par 4 or a par 5, where he needs distance, he may want to "ride" the wind. For instance, if the wind is moving from left to right, he will want to aim left and allow the ball to curve with the wind, giving him more distance. If he doesn't need distance, he may work the ball into the wind to create more backspin, allowing the ball to land softer. This is a particularly good tactic when hitting into greens.

No matter what shot he plays, he must always try to get the ball to the target he selected when he decided on his strategy.

So now he has the ball teed where he wants to and has made his shot selection. He then goes through a preswing routine that allows him to aim, set up, and reach a desired tension level to make his best swing.

Outside Versus Inside Thinking

Once our imaginary player goes through his routine, he then begins to swing. What is he thinking about as he swings? This is a question posed to me a lot. Through my experience with expert players, I find that they tend to think of one of four things, which reflect the organization of this book: (1) target, (2) ball flight, (3) club movement, or (4) body movement.

TARGET. Sam Snead used to play thinking only of the target. Everything he did was done instinctively to get the ball there. To reiterate that point, I'll tell you a story about Sam. He and I were doing a golf school at Pinehurst. Before we started, he asked me what he was supposed to do. I told him that as guest instructor he was to play a hole with the students and then explain how he played it. "That won't work," he said. "Why not?" "Because they can't do it." I said, "Well, do it anyway." The first hole was a short par 4 of about 300 yards with a huge tree right in the middle of the fairway. Sam teed up on the right side of the tee and hit a towering fade that landed just short of the green and then rolled onto the putting surface! He said, "See, none of 'em can do that!" As I watched him and talked with him, I realized that he just looked at the shot and simply got a feeling for what seemed like

EVERYTHING SAM SNEAD DID ON THE GOLF COURSE WAS INSTINCTIVE.

PAYNE STEWART RELIES HEAVILY ON VISUALIZATION TO CREATE HIS SHOT SHAPES.

the best way to play it. Everything he did was instinctive and right-brained. He played draws when they were called for and fades when they looked "right." He never used yardages but just "eyeballed" the distance. I concluded that there was no conscious directive in his mind other than "ball to target."

BALL FLIGHT. The person I know best who thinks mainly of the flight of the ball while swinging is Payne Stewart. He selects his target, then decides what ball flight best suits the shot requirements. Then he instinctively (right brain) makes adjustments to create that ball flight. In fact, when I teach him, I do so by merely having him hit the *opposite* shot of the one that's giving him problems. For instance, if he is getting in front of the ball and hitting low fades, I'll just ask him to do the opposite ("Hit high draws, Payne") until his swing becomes *balanced*. The key here is that I don't tell him how to hit high draws. I just ask him to do it. Consequently, he visualizes a target and adjusts his position until he "feels" as if he can hit a high draw. In fact, when he and I play, he always describes where the ball will start and finish. I once tried to simplify his swing by making some adjustments. After making them, he told me, "I can't play that way." I said, "Why not?" He said, "The ball goes too straight. I have to work the ball to play well." In fact, Payne's ability to "create" ball flights before he swings makes him much better in relation to his peers on hard shots. He won the U.S. Open in 1991 with two shots that come to mind. On the last day of regulation play at Hazeltine, he hit a ball over and around a huge tree to make a birdie on the 16th hole and picked up two strokes on Scott Simpson. On the last hole, when the tournament outcome was still in doubt, he hit a fairway bunker shot up a hill to win the tournament.

CLUB MOVEMENT. Some golfers play best thinking of what the club is doing. Tom Kite is one of those players. He picks his target, selects his ball flight, then decides what the *club* must do to produce the selected ball flight to the target. Some common thoughts Tom uses: "Take the *club* straight back," "Swing the *club* left after impact," "Cover the ball with the *club*face," "Feel like the *club* is laid off at the top," and so forth. He also uses some body thoughts (see below), but he feels as if he plays best with *club*-movement thoughts. In fact, Tom has used a different set of swing thoughts to produce each of his nineteen Tour victories.

BODY MOVEMENT. A lot of golfers think of what the *body* does to get the *club* to produce the selected *ball flight* to the target. While this may seem a little complicated, it's probably the prevalent mode of thinking among golfers of all levels. For instance, Nick Faldo seems to play golf this way. I've watched his caddie, Fanny Sunesson, spend hours on the driving range holding Nick's right *knee* in place while he starts his downswing to help him eliminate sliding of the *hips,* a problem he has. I've seen his coach, David Leadbetter, cock Nick's *wrists* up while turning his left *shoulder* under his *chin.* All of these cues make a player *body*-conscious while swinging.

TOM KITE WOULD RATHER THINK OF WHAT THE CLUB IS DOING IN THE SWING THAN OF WHAT THE BALL WILL BE DOING DURING ITS FLIGHT.

NICK FALDO CONCENTRATES ON WHAT HIS BODY SHOULD BE DOING THROUGHOUT THE SWING.

There is no right or wrong way to think while swinging, just as there is no right or wrong way to swing. *There is just your way.*

Which way should *you* think? A lot depends on your current ability. Those who think of target or ball flight while swinging are generally *product* (or external) thinkers. Those who think club or body movement are *process* (or internal) thinkers. Generally, product thinkers are more feel-oriented (right brain), while process thinkers are generally more analytical (left brain) in nature.

Obviously, if you could think of nothing but the target, all would be simpler, but such thinking is effective only if the ball goes there. I've seen a lot of pseudo psychologists tell their students to just *react* to the *target* and not to think about the golf swing, and no matter how hard they thought "target," they still topped the ball! If you've played a lot of golf and you're adept at controlling your ball, then it's possible to think "target" and have the ball go there, but if you don't have control over the flight of the ball, then you need to be a process thinker. Therefore, product thinking is the province of a very small number of players.

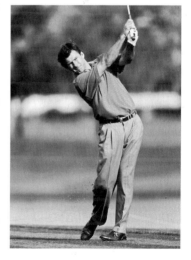

So now we've teed off. We get ready for our next shot and we go through *exactly* the same process. That is, strategy for target, visualizing ball flight, preswing routine, and in-swing cueing.

For instance, playing into the green means aiming at the fat part of the green and then curving the ball toward the pin from there. That includes strategy and visualizing ball flight, then going through your preswing routine and mentally cueing your swing and then moving on to the next shot. That's really all there is to balanced golf!

After the round, the balanced player will go to the range and work on the shots that gave him trouble on the course. This could take a long time or a short time, depending on how long it takes the player to solve his problem shot or shots.

THE THREE USABLE BALL FLIGHTS.

THE BALANCED BALL FLIGHT

A ball in flight (or on the ground) has three main dimensions:

1. Direction.

2. Trajectory.

3. Distance.

CONTROL
SHORT CLUBS

DISTANCE
LONG CLUBS

FADE BALANCED DRAW

Other dimensions include spin axis and spin rate, which we will cover while discussing direction, trajectory, and distance. Let's take direction first.

Direction

There are three usable ball flights in golf: (1) the straight shot (one that starts, flies, and ends in line with the target), (2) the draw (or hook) shot (for a right-handed golfer, a shot that starts right of the target and curves left back toward the target), and (3) the fade (or slice) shot (for a right-handed golfer, a shot that starts left of the target and curves right toward the target). Each of these three shots has different properties.

THE STRAIGHT SHOT. The straight shot is the *balanced* ball flight. You've undoubtedly heard lots of stories about the straight shot being the "hardest one to hit," or "no one really hits a straight shot," or "a straight shot will kill you every time!" But while the majority of Tour players may favor a certain shape to their "plain vanilla" shots, most of them hit the ball so straight you'd be hard-pressed to see much, if any, curve. The straight shot is the most efficient shot for several reasons.

First, there is no glance to the hit. To hit a straight shot, the club must be traveling toward the target and with the face looking at the target when the ball leaves the club. Therefore, the ball is evenly compressed and the only spin is true underspin. That's why Tour players create so much stopping action on their iron shots: they hit the ball so squarely there is no sidespin, only backspin.

Second, the shortest distance between two points is a straight line (or straight shot). Therefore, a lot of the energy of the shot is not wasted by leaving the target line and then coming back to it.

The other two usable shots have different but effective properties when used correctly. But all curves are glancing blows and therefore less efficient.

THE DRAW (OR HOOK) SHOT. We'll call this shot a draw because a hook is simply a big draw. Or as the late Bert Yancey once said, "A draw is just a nice word for a hook." This shot is preferred by people who need distance. The reason this shot generally produces extra length is that the clubface is looking to the left of the direction in which the club is swinging. This closed or closing clubface spins the ball on an axis that produces less backspin than a straight shot does. Therefore, the less backspin results in less "drag" in flight and more roll on the ground, thus more distance.

Also, to start this shot to the right of the target (to allow for the curve to the left), the path of the swing is generally more to the right, or from inside the target line to outside it. This inside-out path is usually more shallow in approach to the ball, which reduces backspin as well. This shallow angle of approach also makes it easier to hit long clubs that have less loft, such as the woods or long irons.

So people who need distance should try to favor a draw shape to their shots. Players currently on the PGA Tour who favor this shot are Tom Kite, Ben Crenshaw, and Mark O'Meara, all of whom are small in stature and need the distance-enhancing help this shot offers. In fact, it's been documented that as players get older, they turn to drawing the ball for distance. Jack Nicklaus, Lee Trevino, and Dave Stockton, who were all faders of the ball on the regular PGA Tour, added the draw as they reached the Senior PGA Tour.

THE FADE (OR SLICE) SHOT. We'll call this shot a fade because a slice is simply a big fade. Or as Bert Yancey also said, "A fade is just a nice word for a slice." This shot is preferred by people who have lots of distance but need control. This shot produces more control because the clubface must be open or opening to the path on which you are swinging. This open clubface produces more loft than you would normally have, thus increasing backspin and decreasing sidespin. Therefore, this shot will land softer, meaning less roll. Also, to start this shot to the left (to allow for the curve to the right), the club's path will generally be to the left—or outside the target line to inside the target line, or outside in. This outside-in angle is generally steeper, which also contributes to the increased backspin.

The outside-in path is particularly good for hitting shorter clubs, which require a steeper angle. In fact, even if you play a draw for distance with your long game, you need to play more of a fade for your short game—most short-game mistakes come from having too much hook in your swing. For example, if your swing is moving inside out, the face of the club must close to hit the ball on line, therefore reducing loft and backspin. That is not very conducive to hitting a soft shot over a bunker! Also, the shallow, inside-out path of the hook swing brings the club very close to the ground behind the ball, making "fat" shots (the club striking the turf behind the ball) and "thin" shots (the club striking the ball near its equator) more likely.

Finally, making an inside-out swing with the face closing moves the hosel out toward the ball, increasing the possibility of shanks and heeled shots. Not one of these sounds like a very good option, does it? So, if you don't hit a straight shot around the green, then hit a "cut" shot (another name for a little fade).

Players on the PGA Tour who use a fade as their standard ball flight include Tiger Woods, Fred Couples, and Davis Love III. All are long hitters looking for control and are willing to sacrifice distance.

Trajectory

Trajectory is the height to which you hit the ball. I mention it second because when you get direction and trajectory perfectly balanced, factoring distance becomes easier.

Let's call the *balanced* trajectory *medium* height; anything higher, *high;* anything lower, *low.* A ball goes lower when the clubface is closed or when the handle leans toward the target, ahead of the clubhead. This is known as "hooding" the clubface. The ball goes higher when the clubface is open or when the handle is farther away from the target than the clubhead is. This is known as "laying back" the clubface. (See photos.)

LEANING THE HANDLE OF THE CLUB FORWARD (TOWARD THE TARGET) WILL GENERALLY CAUSE THE CLUBFACE TO BE HOODED, RESULTING IN A LOWER TRAJECTORY. HOWEVER, CLOSING THE CLUBFACE ALSO PRODUCES A LOWER TRAJECTORY AND A DRAW.

LEANING THE HANDLE OF THE CLUB BACKWARD (AWAY FROM THE TARGET) WILL GENERALLY CAUSE THE CLUBFACE TO BE LAID BACK, RESULTING IN A HIGHER TRAJECTORY AND A FADE. HOWEVER, OPENING THE CLUBFACE WILL ALSO CAUSE A HIGHER TRAJECTORY AND A FADE.

When the trajectory is a medium (balanced) height, the actual height the ball travels is then determined by how fast the club is moving. But regardless of that, you should strive to make *all* clubs go the same height! (See drawing.)

As you can see, even though the pitching wedge starts out higher, it ends up going shorter because it "peaks" out earlier. The 6-iron (and all clubs in between) starts out lower. However, due to the increased clubhead speed produced by the longer shaft, it goes longer but reaches the same "peak" farther downrange. Ditto with the driver. For this to happen, however, you must have a corresponding increase in velocity with each club. A person who swings the club slower will not be able to "peak" out the longer clubs as high as a player who swings the club faster. The slower swinger does not generate enough clubhead speed to produce the backspin necessary to create the lift to hit the long clubs high. That's why you so often hear of long hitters who hit the ball high (John Daly and Tiger Woods) and, in particular, the long irons high (Jack Nicklaus in his prime). That's also the reason a lot of women, seniors, and weaker players reach a point with their irons when a longer club doesn't go any farther than the one preceding it.

EACH CLUB'S BALL FLIGHT SHOULD PEAK AT THE SAME HEIGHT.

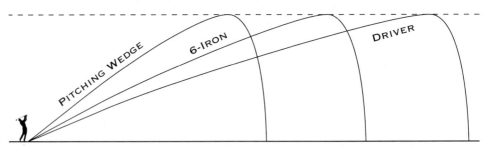

The late Claude Harmon told me that Ben Hogan believed so strongly in a similar trajectory for all clubs that he found a tree at Seminole Golf Club in Jupiter, Florida (where he did his winter practice), which was the height he wanted on his shots. So he would start with his pitching wedge and make the ball peak at the top of that tree. Then he would move back 10 yards or so and make his 9-iron peak at the top of the tree, and so on through the clubs in his bag until he could make all the clubs peak at the same height. He believed this trajectory control was the best way to predict the distance his shots would travel.

Obviously, there are times when you don't want the medium-height shot. Sometimes you want to hit the ball *low*. For instance, if you are a short hitter, your ball will go lower naturally. If you play golf in a place that has a lot of wind, you'll want a lower ball flight. Lee Trevino, who grew up in Texas, and Paul Azinger, who grew up in Florida, both hit lower-than-normal ball flights. In addition, you'll find a number of courses that are flat in those two states, producing fairways that allow the ball to roll a lot, thus rewarding a lower shot.

There are times when a higher-than-normal shot is more desirable as well. For instance, when the fairways are very soft and don't allow roll, you want to carry the ball in the air as far as possible. Also, hilly courses, as well as elevated or very hard greens, require a higher ball flight that lands softly. Jack Nicklaus and Tom Weiskopf both grew up in Ohio, where success depends on that type of shot.

Distance

Here the balanced ball flight is *correct* distance, not necessarily greater distance. Obviously, you would not prefer distance that goes beyond the target or is short of the target. At the 1984 PGA Championship at Cherry Hills in Denver, Hal Sutton was playing with one of my students. On the 17th hole, a par 5 with an island-style green, Hal, who hits the ball low, tried reaching the green in two on each of the first two days. In the first round, the ball hit the bank short of the green and came back in the water. In the second round, he flew the ball five yards farther, but the flight was so low the ball bounded over the green. After the second round, Hal came to me and said that my student had recommended I give him a short-game lesson. I told Hal I thought he needed to change his full swing. He said, "I'm the longest straight-hitter on tour." I said, "You don't want to be the longest in yardage, but the most correct." He never did take that short-game lesson!

It might seem as if maximum distance on your full shots would be the best option. But that could be a false assumption. There are a number of players who have worked on reducing the distance their shots travel. Nick Faldo was a very long hitter before working with David Leadbetter to make his swing better designed for major tournaments, which place a greater premium on control. The same could be said for Curtis Strange and Davis Love III. Their success would certainly point to the need for *balance* between distance and control. In my opinion, John Daly will have to make those changes. Phil Mickelson has started making them and has had startling results. There are any number of players who have increased their distance and become better. Tom Kite and Corey Pavin are a couple of examples I know pretty well!

So in selecting a swing style, understand that there are balancing considerations when choosing distance. As a general rule, the ability to hit the ball a long way is a tremendous advantage. Just look at the facts: There is an increasing group of players in the superlong category doing well. Such established stars as Greg Norman, Davis Love III, John Daly, and others have all been ranked in the Top 10 in driving distance at one time or another. And Tiger Woods hits it past all of them. The reason they do so well? Because of their extra distance, they can use clubs that are more forgiving off the tee and still have a distance advantage going into the green. Consequently, they use more "scoring" clubs than an average or below-average hitter does.

However, the only length that is useful is controlled length.

THE BALANCED MOVEMENT
OF THE CLUB

To make the ball go toward the target, the club must be moving correctly at impact. Regarding impact, there are five factors that determine where the ball goes:

1. The position of the clubface.

2. The path of the clubhead.

3. The angle of approach of the clubhead.

4. The speed of the clubhead.

5. The contact point of the ball on the clubface.

SQUARE FACE

CLOSED FACE

OPEN FACE

The Position of the Clubface

Let's review the principles of clubface alignment when the club meets the ball. At impact, the clubface can be pointing at the target (square), to the left of the target (closed), or to the right of the target (open). If the clubface is looking to the left of the direction in which the club is swinging (the path), the ball will curve to the left (a hook). If the clubface is looking to the right of the direction in which the club is swinging, the ball will curve to the right (a slice). If the clubface is looking in the same direction as the path of the club, the ball will go in that direction. So if the club is swinging to the right and the clubface is square to that path, the ball will go straight to the right; and likewise, if the club is swinging to the left and the clubface is square to that path, the ball will go straight to the left. As you can see, the position of the clubface has the most to do with the direction of the shot.

To understand how the clubface works during the benchmark (or balanced) swing, I relate the following: The clubface starts square to the target line. As the club goes back, it continues to face the ball until the club is at about 8:30 on an imaginary clockface (9 o'clock is parallel to the ground). Then, as the right arm begins to fold, the clubface starts to open. After the right arm begins to fold, the right wrist starts to cock until the clubface is 90 degrees open to the arc on which it is swinging. It remains in this 90-degree-open position until the club is about waist-high on the downswing. Then it begins to close until it is square when the ball leaves the clubface. The clubface remains square to where the ball was until the left arm begins to fold, and it continues closing as the left wrist bends until it is 90 degrees closed to the arc on which it is swinging (see photos on pages 44–45). To prove the point that this is a benchmark swing for reference only, I would tell you that Tom Kite's clubface works like this, but Payne Stewart's

*"You can hit
down a little with
the irons and up
a little with the
driver."*
—HARVEY PENICK

clubface is closed to these positions and Corey Pavin's clubface is open!

The Path of the Clubhead

Let's review the principles of the swing path. At impact, the clubhead can be swinging toward the target, to the left of the target, or to the right of the target. The primary importance of the swing path is what it requires of the clubface position to make the ball go to the target. If the swing path is toward the target, then the clubface must be square to the target, producing a straight shot. If the swing path is to the left of the target, the clubface must be open to this path so that the ball will curve toward the target (a slice). If the swing path is to the right of the target, the clubface must be closed to this path so that the ball will curve toward the target (a hook).

To describe the path of the benchmark (or balanced) swing, I relate the following: The swing path is determined by the club you are using. The angle at which the shaft extends from the clubhead (called the lie of the club) describes the angle at which the club goes back and comes through the ball. On the takeaway, the club goes back and up at this angle. The club stays at this angle until the right elbow starts to fold. This folding of the right elbow takes the club above this angle (or plane) all the way to the top of the swing. On the downswing, the club will start to flatten from the top-of-the-backswing position until it gets back onto the original angle at about waist-high in the downswing. It then remains at that angle through impact and after, until the left arm begins to fold, when it again moves above that angle until the finish.

The Angle of Approach of the Clubhead

What we mean by the angle of approach is the angle at which the clubhead is moving related to the ball and the ground. The club can strike the ball at the bottom of the swing, when the club is moving level with the ground, or it can hit the ball while the club is moving downward, or it can hit the ball while the club is moving upward. While the following is not an exactly true statement, its general concept is often useful in explaining the angle of approach. For a proficient player, there is a "flat spot" about the length of a dollar bill in the bottom of the swing due to the shifting of the player's weight and the releasing of the clubhead. As a general rule, it is best to hit your irons at the back of that dollar bill, to hit your fairway woods in the middle of that dollar bill, and to hit your driver at the front of that dollar bill.

Here is how the angle of approach is created in the benchmark (or balanced) swing: As the club is traveling down the plane line, the body is positioned so that its center is behind the ball. The left shoulder is even with the front of the "dollar bill." With an iron, the club moves down and through the ball, then creates a divot where the dollar bill would be. The depth of the divot is determined by the uprightness of the club: the more upright the club, the deeper the divot; the flatter the club, the shallower the divot. With a driver and the ball on a tee, the club goes through the flat spot and catches the ball at the end of the dollar bill. With a fairway wood, contact occurs in the middle of the dollar bill. That point of contact is created by the ball position at address, not by a change in the swing.

THINK OF THE BOTTOM OF THE SWING ARC AS A FLAT SPOT ABOUT THE LENGTH OF A DOLLAR BILL. HIT YOUR IRONS AT THE BACK OF THE DOLLAR BILL, YOUR DRIVER AT THE FRONT OF IT.

The Speed of the Clubhead

Here we are talking about the speed at which the clubhead is moving at impact. Obviously, the club can be moving at the right speed to go to the target, have too much speed, or have too little. As a general rule, there are two different ways to create clubhead speed. The first is through muscular effort, or hitting. The second is through centrifugal force, or swinging.

Hitting is best used by strong but inflexible people. It is created by cocking the arms and wrists and then uncocking them, using muscle power to get clubhead speed. Hitters on the PGA Tour include Craig Stadler and Dan Pohl.

Swinging is best used by flexible people. It is created by the rotation of the body, with the arms and club being "flung" through the hitting area. Swingers on the PGA Tour include Payne Stewart and Davis Love III.

"Ben Hogan was the best hitter *I ever saw, but nobody could* swing *like Ben [Crenshaw]."*
—HARVEY PENICK

"A toe-deep divot can come when that face is either open or closed, not just when your hands are high."

—HARVEY PENICK

Perhaps the best way to imagine the difference in these two styles is to imagine the difference betwen a shot-putter and a discus-thrower. A shot-putter pushes the shot through brute force, and a discus-thrower flings the discus. Here's another way to look at it: think of a boxer (a hitter) stepping into a punch, and a karate expert (a swinger) rotating his hips and throwing his legs for a kick; or in football, a straight-on placekicker (a hitter) versus a soccer-style kicker (a swinger).

The Contact Point of the Ball on the Clubface

No matter what the significance of the previous four impact factors, they are predictable only with solid contact. We define that as the point on the club-face where the ball is struck and the club doesn't twist, or the "sweet spot." If club/ball contact is toward the toe of an iron, the club will open and the ball will go to the right. If contact is toward the heel of an iron, the heel will back up, closing the clubface and sending the ball to the left. If the contact is toward the bottom of the club, the ball will go lower; if toward the top, the ball will go higher. The ball will fly shorter in almost all these instances. Of course, the benchmark (or balanced) point of contact is in this sweet spot of the clubface.

Here is a chart to help you determine how the factors interact.

MOVEMENT OF THE CLUB

	STRAIGHT (BENCHMARK)	HOOK	SLICE
POSITION OF CLUBFACE	Square	Closed to path	Open to path
PATH OF CLUBHEAD	Straight	Inside out	Outside in
ANGLE OF APPROACH OF CLUBHEAD	Level	Level to up	Level to down
SPEED OF CLUBHEAD	Right amount	Needs less	Needs more
CONTACT POINT OF BALL ON CLUBFACE	Solid	Solid toward heel	Solid toward toe

THE BALANCED MOVEMENT OF THE BODY

At the beginning of this chapter, I started by talking about the balanced mental game to get the ball to the target. Then I talked about the balanced ball flight to get the ball to the target. Next I talked about the balanced movement of the club to get the ball to the target. Now, finally, I'll talk about the balanced movement of the *body* to make the club get the ball to the target.

There are three areas I will discuss in this chapter: the overall body, the arms, and the hands and wrists. I will explain (1) how these parts work, (2) their sequence of movement, and (3) how the parts start.

How These Parts Work

THE OVERALL BODY. When I talk about the body, I mean the head, neck, shoulders, torso, hips, legs, and feet. The body in a correct golf swing works

"If I have a fault, it's that I let my students move their head too much, but I'd rather have that than having it too still."

—HARVEY PENICK

like a kitchen door. On the backswing, it opens; on the downswing, it closes; and on the follow-through, it opens again. Like a kitchen door, it has a doorjamb with hinges. The doorjamb is the spine, and the hinges are the shoulders and hips. As you make your backswing, your shoulders and hips turn around your spine to your right. This places most of your weight on your right side. You want to *turn* to get your weight shifted to your right, not move laterally. Into your downswing and follow-through, your body turns around your spine until it is facing left of your target. As you do this, most of your weight goes to your left. Again, you want to *turn* to get your weight shifted to your left, not move laterally.

"I don't tell people to cock their wrists, because they always do it wrong."
—HARVEY PENICK

THE ARMS. Your arms should swing naturally. On the backswing, the right elbow cocks while the left arm remains extended. The right elbow remains in front of and pointing toward the right hip. There is no conscious turning of the arms, just the folding of the right elbow. This move is simply reversed on the downswing until both arms are straight about a foot and a half past impact; then the left arm begins to fold, remaining in front of the left hip and pointed at the left hip while the right arm remains extended. Once again, there is no conscious rolling of the arms, just a cocking, uncocking, and recocking.

"I like players with those lively hands."
—HARVEY PENICK

THE HANDS AND WRISTS. The hands and wrists work naturally as well. They work just as if you were going to throw a baseball with your right hand. At address, the right wrist is flat and the left wrist is bent. On the backswing, the right wrist bends backward until the left wrist is flat. Since this is the hand position you want to be in at impact, there is no change in the hand until halfway through the follow-through, where the left wrist bends and the right wrist flattens. Just as with the arms, there is no conscious effort to turn the hands on the backswing, downswing, or follow-through.

"The first move starting down is when your weight goes to your left foot and your right arm comes into your side."
—HARVEY PENICK

Their Sequence of Movement

The sequence (or timing) of the parts is very important to consistent ball-striking. In both the backswing and the downswing, the sequence is (1) body, (2) arms, and (3) wrists. The complete movement goes like this: On the backswing, the shoulders start to turn while the arms, hands, and wrists remain in the same relationship to the body until about 8:30 (halfway back is 9 o'clock). Then the right arm begins to fold, which starts to open the clubface. Then the right wrist begins to bend backward until the left wrist is flat. At the top of the swing, the shoulders have turned 90 degrees, the right arm has bent 90 degrees, and the wrists have cocked at least 90 degrees.

On the downswing, the right shoulder begins to move down and out toward the ball, forcing the left hip over the left foot. The arms and wrists retain their angles. This continues until the right elbow is in front of the right hip. At this point, the right arm begins to straighten and the hips square the club.

At impact, the shoulders are open, the hips are open, the right wrist is still bent, and the left wrist is flat. After impact, both arms straighten about a foot and a half past the ball. The left arm begins to fold in front of the left hip. At the halfway-through position, the left wrist begins to bend and the right wrist flattens. In the finish, the right shoulder has passed the left, the right hip has passed the left, the arms have remained in front of the body, and the club is behind the head.

How the Parts Start

The setup is the most important part of the golf swing because everything else reacts to it. If you were poorly aimed, you wouldn't want a good swing, because the ball would never go toward the target. The same thing is true of spine angle, posture, and grip. People often ask how far I can take them, and I respond that three of my students have won U.S. Opens! They then ask how fast I can take them, and I always respond that I can teach as fast as they can learn! What this means is that you have to learn things in the sequence in which they occur in the swing. If you start poorly, you'll have to make adjustments to hit the ball to the target. Same for the backswing, downswing, and so forth. Here we go.

For the body to work correctly, the positioning of the spine is most critical. First, the spine should be reasonably straight. It's like an axle on a car; a bent axle creates a wobbly ride. Second, your spine should be aimed at the ball. Let me explain that. If you remember the movement-of-the-club section, I talked there about the lie angle of the club creating the path of the

1. ADDRESS.

2. BACKSWING AT 8:30.

3. TWO-THIRDS OF THE WAY BACK.

4. AT THE TOP.

5. FLAT LEFT WRIST.

6. HALFWAY DOWN.

THE
BENCHMARK
SWING

7. IMPACT.

8. HIPS MORE OPEN THAN SHOULDERS.

9. HALFWAY THROUGH.

10. FINISH.

11. RIGHT SHOULDER LOWER THAN LEFT.

AT ADDRESS,
YOUR SPINE
SHOULD BE AT A
RIGHT ANGLE TO
THE CLUBSHAFT.

POSTURE THAT
IS TOO UPRIGHT
CAUSES AN
OVER-THE-TOP
MOVE.

POSTURE THAT
IS TOO BENT
OVER CAUSES A
SEVERELY
INSIDE-OUT
SWING PATH.

swing. Because of that, the spine must be at a right angle to the lie angle. This makes all of your power go at the ball. If your spine is too straight up, all of your power will be above the ball; and if your spine is too bent over, all of your power will go inside the ball. (See photos.) You also want to align your body parallel to the target line.

For the arms to work correctly, two things should be in place. First, the left arm should hang straight down from the shoulder. If you reach too much for the ball, your swing will tend to come inside too early; and if your arms are tucked too close to your body, your swing will tend to go outside too much. Second, because the left hand is higher on the club than the right hand is, the

YOU SHOULD FEEL A REVERSE-K POSITION AT ADDRESS.

left shoulder should be higher than the right shoulder. This tilt is created by shifting the hips slightly toward the target, creating a reverse-K look. The flat spot in the swing occurs between the left cheek and the left armpit. Consequently, the position of the ball for irons should be under the left cheek; for the fairway woods, under the left pocket; and for the driver, under the left armpit. The insides of the feet should be even with the shoulders with a driver and correspondingly narrower until the outsides of the feet are shoulder-width with a wedge.

Finally, for the hands and wrists to work correctly, the grip must be balanced. To hit a straight shot with the left wrist flat at impact, you must have the following grip. If you were to stand up naturally and just let your arms hang at your sides, you would notice that your left hand faces you. This is the same sensation you want with your left-hand grip. When you put your left hand on the club in the facing-you position, place your left thumb about a quarter turn off-center to the right. The heel pad of your left hand should be on top of the grip (not to the side), and the space between your left thumb and the first knuckle of your left forefinger should be closed. Most good players can see two knuckles on the left hand at address. The reason the thumb needs to be toward the back of the grip is because the hands

*"Don't twist
the skin, just
place your hands
on there and
hold it."*

—HARVEY PENICK

will be four inches closer to the target at impact than they were at address, and the thumb needs to be there to square the clubface.

The right hand should be placed so it faces the same direction as the clubface. It shouldn't face the ground or the sky to any degree. The lifeline of the right hand slips over the left thumb, and the gap between the right thumb and the first knuckle of the right forefinger should be closed.

That is how the benchmark (or balanced) golf swing should look. Now let's start designing your swing for you!

How to Balance Shots That Are Misdirected

HOW TO BALANCE SHOTS THAT CURVE

All shots that curve off-line are caused by the *clubface* looking in a direction different from the one in which the clubhead is swinging. All clubface errors come from either the grip you are using or the position of your lead wrist at impact or both.

> *"Use the grip that squares the face."*
> —HARVEY PENICK

There are three possible grips to use:

Neutral. In a neutral grip, the clubface is aligned with the back of the lead hand.

Weak. Here, the hands are turned more to the left on the handle (for a right-handed golfer).

Strong. The hands are turned more to the right on the handle (for a right-handed golfer).

NEUTRAL GRIP.

WEAK GRIP.

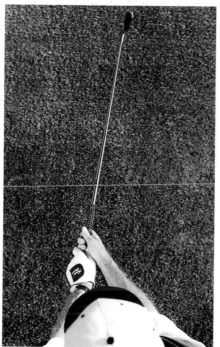

STRONG GRIP.

And there are five impact-wrist positions:

Flat. The back of the lead wrist is flat and the back of the trailing wrist is bent.

Flipped. The lead wrist is bent or cupped and the trailing wrist is flat or bowed.

Bowed. The lead wrist is bowed and the trailing wrist is acutely bent.

Rolled. The lead wrist is flat but rolled to the left.

Reverse rolled. The lead wrist is flat but rolled to the right.

None of the three grips is necessarily wrong as long as it matches a compatible wrist position at impact. Here are the compatible arrangements of grips and wrist positions (all other combinations are incompatible):

Neutral grip + flat wrist position.

Weak grip + flipped or rolled wrist position.

Strong grip + bowed or reverse-rolled wrist position.

FLAT LEFT WRIST.

FLIPPED.

BOWED.

ROLLED.

REVERSE ROLLED.

How to Counterbalance Shots That Slice

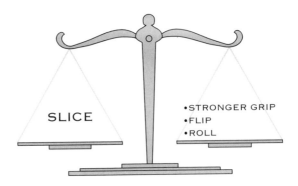

All shots that curve to the right are created by a clubface that looks to the right of the path on which the club is swinging. There are three counterbalances:

STRONGER GRIP. This is the most effective and common correction for an open face at impact. I use this correction 99 percent of the time in my teaching. Most people who play golf have grips that open the face of the club as much as 120 degrees on the backswing, requiring 120 degrees of closing on the downswing and leading to all sorts of gymnastics to square the clubface. If your shots curve to the right (a slice for right-handers), go to Chapter 4 and review the balanced-grip section (pages 47–48). Try to make your grip look like the one in the photographs there. If the ball continues to curve to the right, continue turning your hands to the right on the handle until the ball goes straight or left. *A word of caution:* If you have had a weak grip in the past and move to a neutral or strong grip, your slices may become pulled shots (shots that go straight left of the target with little curve). If this occurs, keep using the new grip and counterbalance the pull with information on pages 57–59 .

TRY THE TWO-TEES DRILL FOR A STRONGER GRIP (SEE PAGE 130).

FLIP. If you have tried strengthening your grip in the past and have not found it a workable solution, learn to uncock your wrists earlier on the downswing until the back of your lead wrist is in a flipped position facing up and to the left of the target at impact. The 1994 Masters champion, José Maria Olazabal, does this (see photo). There are a couple of drawbacks to this correction: An early release in the downswing reduces distance. Also,

JOSÉ MARIA
OLAZABAL FLIPS
HIS LEFT WRIST
TO SQUARE THE
CLUBFACE
THROUGH THE
HITTING AREA.

without other compensating factors, making solid contact is tough unless the ball is in an exceptional lie. Finally, this action tends to hit the ball high.

TRY THE TEE-TO-RETEE DRILL FOR AN EARLIER RELEASE (SEE PAGE 131).

ROLL. A third and more often used correction to hit the ball straight with a weak grip is the rolled release, so that the back of the lead wrist is turned to the left at impact, even though the wrist is flat. Corey Pavin plays this way. He has tried to change his grip, but found a stronger grip too awkward to use. Consequently, he rolls his forearms to the left through impact until the clubface is square.

TRY THE WRISTWATCH DRILL FOR A ROLLED RELEASE (SEE PAGE 132).

How to Counterbalance Shots That Hook

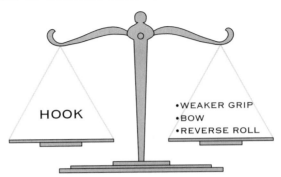

HOOK

- WEAKER GRIP
- BOW
- REVERSE ROLL

All shots that curve to the left are created by a clubface that looks to the left of the path on which the club is swinging. There are three counterbalances:

WEAKER GRIP. While this is an option I use occasionally to stop a hook, it can be disastrous if overdone, so do it a little at a time. In fact, in all the time I watched Harvey Penick teach, I saw him weaken only one player's left-hand grip. That was a club member named Ed Turley. Ed's left-hand grip was turned so far to the right you could see all five knuckles! Harvey told Ed, "If you keep turning that left-hand grip to the right, eventually you'll have it back where it belongs." Try moving your grip to the left until it reaches the neutral position (see page 51). Once it reaches neutral, *do not* move it to the weak position. Use one of the following corrections—the bow or the reverse roll—first.

TRY THE TWO-TEES DRILL FOR A WEAKER GRIP (SEE PAGE 130).

BOW. A good method to help you fight off a hook produced by a strong grip is to hit balls with your hands well in advance of the clubhead, causing your lead wrist to be in a bowed position at impact. This will effectively "block out" the hook while producing a lower ball flight. Lee Trevino plays golf this way. The lower ball flight makes this system hard to use if you want height on your long irons and driver.

TRY THE CHIP-PUNCH DRILL FOR A BOWED WRIST AT IMPACT (SEE PAGE 133).

REVERSE ROLL. A good method to use to fight a hook if you need more height is to feel as if you keep your right hand in an "underhanded" position through impact. This keeps the clubface square and allows you to use the loft of the club. Payne Stewart and Paul Azinger play this way.

TRY THE HULA HOOP DRILL FOR A REVERSE ROLL (SEE PAGE 134).

How to Balance Shots That Go Straight but Off-Line

Most of the time, if a ball goes relatively straight but off-line (a push or a pull), the clubface is square to the direction of the swing, but the direction of the swing through impact is off-line, either to the right or the left.

How to Counterbalance Shots That Are Pulled

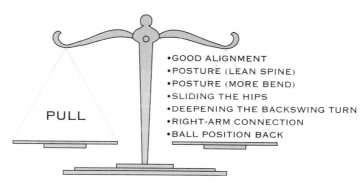

PULL

- GOOD ALIGNMENT
- POSTURE (LEAN SPINE)
- POSTURE (MORE BEND)
- SLIDING THE HIPS
- DEEPENING THE BACKSWING TURN
- RIGHT-ARM CONNECTION
- BALL POSITION BACK

WHEN THE TOP OF THE SPINE IS TOO CLOSE TO THE TARGET, PULLED SHOTS OFTEN RESULT.

GOOD ALIGNMENT. There are rare times when I see a player making a great swing along the wrong alignment. The reason for this rarity is because it normally takes just a short time until the player either corrects the alignment or starts making compensations during the swing for a faulty alignment. I cannot stress this enough: Good alignment is a must fundamental. The correct alignment is one in which the body is square (feet, hips, shoulders parallel) to the target line.

TRY THE TWO-CLUBS DRILL FOR SQUARE ALIGNMENT (SEE PAGE 135).

THE CORRECT SPINE TILT.

POSTURE (LEAN SPINE). If your body turns around your spine, which it does in a proper golf swing, then obviously the position of the spine is crucial. Often when a player is swinging to the left, the top of the spine is set up closer to the target than the bottom of the spine is (see drawing). To get the turn to swing the club on the correct path, the bottom of the spine should be closer to the target than the top of the spine is (see drawing).

TRY THE LEFT-SIDE-AGAINST-WALL DRILL FOR CORRECT SPINE TILT (SEE PAGE 135).

A POSTURE THAT IS TOO VERTICAL ALSO CAUSES PULLED SHOTS.

POSTURE (MORE BEND). Because your body turns around your spine in a proper swing, the angle at which it is bent is critical to swinging on a correct path. A lot of players who swing to the left of the target have positioned the spine too vertically (see drawing). This causes the right shoulder to swing too high, creating that "over the top" move you hear about so often. The correct posture is identified on page 46.

TRY THE TILT-THE-T DRILL FOR CORRECT POSTURE (SEE PAGE 136).

SLIDING THE HIPS. When the club is delivered to the ball on the correct path, it is sometimes referred to as the "slot." With all good players, this slot position is one in which the right elbow is very close to the right hip halfway into the downswing. A number of players, however, in an effort to develop more power or to hit the ball higher, allow the right elbow to leave the side by quite a distance, producing an upright swing. For the elbow to return to the slot, the hips must stay square as the weight shifts to the left. This allows the elbow to return to the slot before the hips rotate to the left on the downswing. If the hips rotate before the elbow returns to the slot, the path of the swing is generally to the left. So, from the top of the backswing, the hips slide laterally toward the target, moving the bottom of the spine closer to the target and dropping the path into an inside-out (to the right) position. Jack Nicklaus plays this way.

TRY THE THREE-BALL-GATE DRILL FOR CORRECT HIP SLIDE (SEE PAGE 137).

DEEPENING THE BACKSWING TURN. Here is a common mistake made by a lot of players: When they begin the backswing, the right shoulder goes *up* rather than *back,* which doesn't allow the club to be in a position at the top of the swing that is far enough to the inside. They tilt instead of turn. This makes it very difficult for the club to come into the ball from inside the target line. The feeling should be that the right shoulder goes behind you, and it will probably feel "flat," or more nearly horizontal to the ground. From there the right shoulder goes toward the ball, pulling the arms and club on that path.

TRY THE JUMP-ROPE DRILL TO TURN, NOT TILT (SEE PAGE 138).

RIGHT-ARM CONNECTION. Often the shoulder goes back correctly but the arms separate from the turn too much, causing too upright a swing, which will produce a path too much to the left. A simple correction is to *feel* as if the right arm stays closer to the side. In actuality, this will put the hands

"I don't like to tell people to come from the inside. They end up pushing it out to the right. I don't see as well as I used to, but when I see that 'chicken wing,' I know where to look for it [right]."

—HARVEY PENICK

over the tip of the right shoulder at the top of the swing, rather than some-where between the shoulder and the ear.

TRY THE HEADCOVER-UNDER-RIGHT-ARM DRILL FOR BETTER CONNECTION (SEE PAGE 139).

BALL POSITION BACK. In the balanced swing, the correct path goes from inside the target line on the backswing to on the target line at impact back to the inside on the follow-through (see drawing). Sometimes a player can make a swing like this but have the ball positioned too far forward in the stance, thereby catching the ball after the club starts swinging back to the left. Playing the ball back in the stance encourages an impact from inside the target line.

TRY THE VARIABLE-BALL-POSITION DRILL FOR CORRECT BALL POSITION (SEE PAGE 139).

THE CORRECT SWING PATH:
INSIDE TO ALONG THE TARGET LINE
TO BACK INSIDE.

"Getting your posture is like the first move to sitting down."
—HARVEY PENICK

How to Counterbalance Shots That Are Pushed

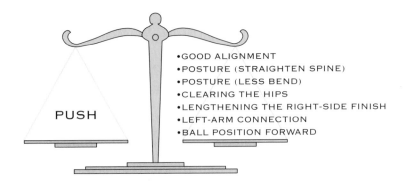

PUSH

- GOOD ALIGNMENT
- POSTURE (STRAIGHTEN SPINE)
- POSTURE (LESS BEND)
- CLEARING THE HIPS
- LENGTHENING THE RIGHT-SIDE FINISH
- LEFT-ARM CONNECTION
- BALL POSITION FORWARD

WHEN THE BOTTOM OF THE SPINE IS TOO CLOSE TO THE TARGET, PUSHED SHOTS OFTEN RESULT.

THE CORRECT SPINE TILT.

A POSTURE THAT IS TOO HORIZONTAL CAUSES PUSHED SHOTS.

GOOD ALIGNMENT. As I said in the section relating to pulled shots, I've rarely seen a player make great swings along the wrong alignment. Poor alignment makes the ball go in the wrong direction, so either the alignment must change or manipulations of the club must be made during the swing. Good alignment is a sound fundamental that only encourages a sound swing. The orthodox alignment is one in which the body is aligned square (or parallel) to the target line.

TRY THE RIGHT-ARM, LEFT-ARM DRILL FOR SOLID ALIGNMENT (SEE PAGE 140).

POSTURE (STRAIGHTEN SPINE). If your body turns around your spine, as it should in a proper swing, then the position of your spine is crucial. Many times, if the player is swinging to the right, the bottom of the spine is set up much closer to the target than the top of the spine is (see drawing). To get the turn to swing the club on the correct path, the backward lean of the top of the spine should be no more than 5 degrees (see drawing).

TRY THE TRIPOD DRILL FOR LESS TILT (SEE PAGE 142).

POSTURE (LESS BEND). If your body turns around your spine, as it should in a proper swing, then the angle at which it is bent is critical to swinging on a correct path. Many players who swing to the right of the target are too bent over and too far from the ball (see drawing). This causes the right shoulder to drop "under" too much, delivering the club on a path too much from the inside. The correct bend at the hips is 45 degrees, and you should stand just far enough from the ball so that your arms hang straight down at address.

TRY THE QUARTERBACK-SNAP DRILL FOR PROPER POSTURE (SEE PAGE 141).

CLEARING THE HIPS. All good players come into the ball with the right elbow close to the right hip. Ideally, once the right elbow is in front of the right hip, the hips should turn to the left, more commonly called "clearing" the hips. A player who makes a backswing whereby the right elbow doesn't get too far from the right hip needs to clear the hips sooner. If the hips slide too far, the club will swing on a path to the right.

TRY THE CHAIR-BY-LEFT-LEG DRILL TO CLEAR THE HIPS (SEE PAGE 143).

LENGTHENING THE RIGHT-SIDE FINISH. There are times when a player might clear the hips correctly but the upper body hangs back, creating a tilted position of the spine and a swing to the right. A good way to get the upper body through the shot is to make the right shoulder and hip pass the left, finishing closer to the target than the left side does.

TRY THE RIGHT-SIDE-TO-LEFT-FOOT DRILL TO SWING THROUGH THE SHOT (SEE PAGE 144).

LEFT-ARM CONNECTION. There are times, even though the body turns correctly, when the left arm leaves the left side and swings out to the right. For the club to continue around in the desired inside-to-down-the-line-to-back-inside path, the upper left arm must remain connected to the left side.

TRY THE HEADCOVER-UNDER-LEFT-ARM DRILL TO MAINTAIN LEFT-ARM CONNECTION (SEE PAGE 144).

BALL POSITION FORWARD. In the balanced swing, the correct path goes from inside the target line to on the target line to back to the inside. Sometimes a player can make a good swing but have the ball positioned too far back in the stance. This causes the ball to be struck before the club starts to go down the target line. Moving the ball forward in the stance will help to start the ball along the target line instead of to the right.

TRY THE TEES-LEFT-AFTER-IMPACT DRILL FOR CORRECT BALL POSITION (SEE PAGE 145).

How to Balance Shots
That Are Mis-hit

When I speak of shots that are mis-hit, I mean those that are not hit on the "sweet spot" of the club. Harvey Penick called that spot the "no roll spot" of the clubface. What he meant was that the ball rolls off the clubface if it is struck somewhere other than on the sweet spot. On an iron shot hit on the toe of the club, the clubface will open up and the ball will go weaker and to the right. On an iron shot hit on the heel of the club, the clubface will close and the ball will go weaker and to the left. On an iron shot hit below the sweet spot, the face will "back up," adding loft to the club and hitting the ball higher.

On wooden clubs or metal woods, the face is not flat. It is curved (called "bulge"). Due to something called "gear effect," balls hit on the toe will tend

TO MAKE SOLID CONTACT, THINK OF YOUR SWING AS A PERFECT CIRCLE.

"I'd like to teach you to hit the ball from there [forward ball position], but I'm going to have to move that ball back where your swing is."

—HARVEY PENICK

to hook and balls hit on the heel will tend to slice. Bulge helps to counter-act the gear effect.

There are grossly mis-hit shots as well. Obviously, the worst one is the complete miss, or "whiff"! Shots hit way out on the toe will skitter directly to the right. Iron shots that are hit so far on the heel that they contact the hosel (or "shank") of the club will also squirt to the right. Some shots are hit so far on the bottom of the club they are topped because the club contacts the ball above center. Some shots are contacted so far on the top of the club that the club enters the ground before contacting the ball (called fat shots). Off the tee with a wood, these shots are called pop-ups. None of these shots sound very appetizing, so let's go about correcting them.

The best way to understand how mis-hits occur is to imagine a circle with a radius from the center. The ball and the clubhead start on the out-side edge of the circle. The radius is the combination of the left arm and the club itself, and the center of the circle is your spine (see drawing).

To create solid contact, the center has to be in the same place at impact as it was at address, and the radius must be intact. With that picture in your mind, let's talk about correcting mis-hits.

How to Counterbalance Shots Hit on the Toe

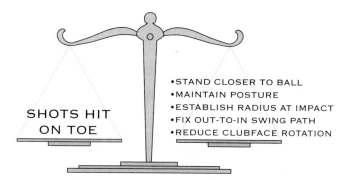

SHOTS HIT
ON TOE

- STAND CLOSER TO BALL
- MAINTAIN POSTURE
- ESTABLISH RADIUS AT IMPACT
- FIX OUT-TO-IN SWING PATH
- REDUCE CLUBFACE ROTATION

STAND CLOSER AT ADDRESS. The most obvious way to correct shots that are hit on the toe is simply to stand closer to the ball at address and make the same swing.

TRY THE ADDRESS-BALL-OFF-HEEL DRILL TO STAND CLOSER (SEE PAGE 145).

MAINTAIN POSTURE THROUGHOUT THE SWING. After you have taken your stance, you should strive to maintain the same posture throughout the swing. If you should pull away from the ball as you swing, a common tendency among many players, you will bring the toe of the club in line with the ball.

TRY THE HALF-SWING DRILL TO FINISH IN THE SAME POSTURE (SEE PAGE 146).

ESTABLISH RADIUS AT IMPACT. If you stand closer to the ball and maintain your posture throughout your swing and you still hit the ball on the toe of the club, then you have shortened your radius at impact. This can happen either by bending your left arm at impact or by bending your left wrist at impact.

TRY THE TEE-IN-FRONT-OF-BALL DRILL FOR LEFT-ARM EXTENSION (SEE PAGE 147).

TRY THE CHIP-PUNCH DRILL FOR A STRAIGHT LEFT WRIST (SEE PAGE 133).

FIX OUT-TO-IN SWING PATH. A common cause of hitting the ball on the toe is the club swinging from outside to inside the target line through impact. Since this is a swing-path problem, check Chapter 5 to review the counterbalances for pulled shots and use those corrections (see pages 57–59).

REDUCE CLUBFACE ROTATION (OPEN TO CLOSE). Even though the posture might be maintained and the radius might be established at impact, the clubface may still contact the ball on the toe because the clubface is closing through impact, causing the toe to get there first. Most of the time this comes from the clubface opening too much on the backswing. So you should strive to reduce that rotation going back so you don't have to rotate it coming through.

TRY THE DOLLAR-BILL-DIVOTS DRILL TO REDUCE CLUBFACE ROTATION (SEE PAGE 148).

How to Counterbalance Shots Hit on the Heel

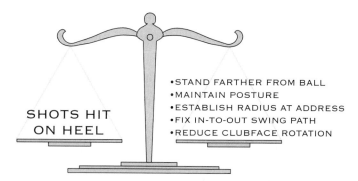

SHOTS HIT
ON HEEL

•STAND FARTHER FROM BALL
•MAINTAIN POSTURE
•ESTABLISH RADIUS AT ADDRESS
•FIX IN-TO-OUT SWING PATH
•REDUCE CLUBFACE ROTATION

STAND FARTHER FROM THE BALL AT ADDRESS. The most logical correction if you are hitting the ball on the heel of the club is simply to stand farther from the ball and make the same swing.

TRY THE ADDRESS-BALL-OFF-TOE DRILL TO ELIMINATE HEELED SHOTS (SEE PAGE 149).

MAINTAIN POSTURE THROUGHOUT THE SWING. While you are swinging, you should strive to maintain your spine angle throughout. If you move closer to the ball as you swing, you will tend to hit it on the heel of the club.

TRY THE CIGAR DRILL FOR CONSISTENT POSTURE (SEE PAGE 150).

ESTABLISH RADIUS AT ADDRESS. Sometimes you can have either your posture too rounded or your arms too slack at address, so when they extend at impact they get longer, thereby causing you to hit the ball on the heel of the club. Getting a good posture and having the correct arm extension at address will enhance your ability to hit solid shots.

TRY THE TAKE-A-BOW DRILL TO MAINTAIN RADIUS (SEE PAGE 151).

FIX IN-TO-OUT SWING PATH. One of the common causes of hitting the ball on the heel of the club, particularly for low handicappers, comes from having the club travel from inside the target line to outside through impact. Since this is a swing-path problem, go to Chapter 5, review the counterbalances for pushed shots, and use those corrections (see pages 60–61).

ELIMINATE CLUBFACE ROTATION. If you maintain your posture and your radius is established at impact, it is still possible to hit the ball on the heel if the clubface is opening through impact. This causes the heel to arrive first, contacting the ball there. The shank, however, actually comes from the clubface being closed at impact. Both problems can be fixed by reducing clubface rotation.

TRY THE ONE-THIRD-BACK-AND-SQUARE-THROUGH DRILL TO ELIMINATE CLUBFACE ROTATION (SEE PAGE 152).

How to Counterbalance Shots Hit on the Bottom

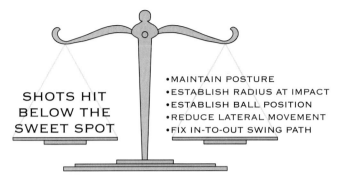

SHOTS HIT
BELOW THE
SWEET SPOT

- MAINTAIN POSTURE
- ESTABLISH RADIUS AT IMPACT
- ESTABLISH BALL POSITION
- REDUCE LATERAL MOVEMENT
- FIX IN-TO-OUT SWING PATH

"Swing the club like you were swinging a grass cutter. Just clip that grass or clip that tee."

—HARVEY PENICK

MAINTAIN POSTURE THROUGHOUT THE SWING. One of the common causes of hitting shots on the bottom of the club comes from straightening up in the swing. A lot of golfers call this "looking up." Once you have established your posture at address, you should strive to maintain the same angle of your spine throughout your swing.

TRY THE DOORJAMB DRILL TO MAINTAIN SPINE ANGLE (SEE PAGE 153).

ESTABLISH RADIUS AT IMPACT. Just as for shots that are hit on the toe of the club, you may maintain your posture throughout your swing but you shorten your radius at impact. This is done by bending your left arm or left wrist.

TRY THE CHIP-PUNCH DRILL TO MAINTAIN RADIUS (SEE PAGE 133).

ESTABLISH BALL POSITION. Another common cause of mis-hitting the ball comes from positioning it incorrectly in the stance. You want to catch the ball in the so-called "flat spot" in the swing, which I describe in Chapter 4 (see page 39). If the ball is too far back in the stance, the club might catch the ball too much on the downswing, hitting it on the bottom of the club. If the ball is too far forward in the stance, the club might catch it on the way up, also hitting it on the bottom of the club.

TRY THE HITTING-BALLS-FROM-A-LINE DRILL TO DETERMINE YOUR BALL POSITION (SEE PAGE 153).

REDUCE LATERAL MOVEMENT. Even though you may have the ball positioned correctly, by moving too laterally you may be in the wrong position to catch the ball solidly. You want to be rotating around your spine, not sliding from side to side.

TRY THE FEET-TOGETHER DRILL TO REDUCE LATERAL MOVEMENT (SEE PAGE 154).

FIX IN-TO-OUT SWING PATH. If your club is moving too much from inside the target line to outside at impact, there will be a tendency to catch the ball on the upswing, creating contact on the bottom of the club (a "thin" shot). Because this is a swing-path problem, go to Chapter 5, review the counterbalances for pushed shots and use those corrections (see pages 60–61).

How to Counterbalance Shots Hit on Top of the Club

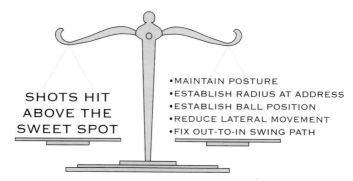

SHOTS HIT ABOVE THE SWEET SPOT

- MAINTAIN POSTURE
- ESTABLISH RADIUS AT ADDRESS
- ESTABLISH BALL POSITION
- REDUCE LATERAL MOVEMENT
- FIX OUT-TO-IN SWING PATH

"You don't have to hit down as much anymore, because these fairways are so good."

—HARVEY PENICK

MAINTAIN POSTURE THROUGHOUT THE SWING. One of the common causes of hitting shots on the top of the club comes from bending over more during your swing than you do at address. Once you have established your posture at address, you should strive to maintain the same angle of your spine throughout your swing.

TRY THE HAND-ON-FOREHEAD DRILL TO MAINTAIN POSTURE (SEE PAGE 155).

ESTABLISH RADIUS AT ADDRESS. Just as for shots that are hit on the heel of the club, you may maintain your posture throughout your swing but at address are too "slack" with your radius. Either you are too "slumped" or your arms are too bent. Paul Runyan, the two-time PGA champion and short-game innovator, calls this "overreaching." As you swing and your arms and wrists extend, the club will go below the ball, causing you to hit it on top of the club.

TRY THE TAKE-A-BOW DRILL TO ESTABLISH YOUR RADIUS (SEE PAGE 151).

ESTABLISH BALL POSITION. Just as with shots that are hit on the bottom of the club, you may have the position of the ball in the wrong place in your stance.

TRY THE HITTING-BALLS-FROM-A-LINE DRILL TO DETERMINE YOUR BALL POSITION (SEE PAGE 153).

REDUCE LATERAL MOVEMENT. Just as with shots hit on the bottom of the club, you may have the position of the ball in the right place but you could be moving too much laterally to catch the ball in the right spot in your swing.

TRY THE FEET-TOGETHER DRILL TO REDUCE LATERAL MOVEMENT (SEE PAGE 154).

FIX OUT-TO-IN SWING PATH. If your club is moving too much from out-side the target line to inside at impact, your swing will approach the ball at too steep an angle, causing the clubhead to go too much underneath the ball. Because this is a swing-path problem, go to Chapter 5, review the counterbalances for pulled shots, and use those corrections (see pages 57–59).

How to Balance Shots That Go the Wrong Height

Generally speaking, the height of a shot is determined by the *effective* loft of the club when the ball leaves the clubface. No matter what the designed loft of the club, it can be altered by adjusting the relationship of the club's handle to the clubhead. The more forward (target side) the handle, the less loft the club will have; the more rearward the handle, the more loft. This is assuming a solid club/ball contact. For example, the handle may be well forward with a driver, but because the clubhead goes underneath the ball, you get a high "pop-up." Or with an iron, the handle may be rearward, but because the clubhead is moving up, the ball may be contacted above its center, thereby causing a topped or "bladed" shot low to the ground.

These conditions are covered in Chapter 6. Also, a clubface that is open will send the ball higher and a clubface that is closed will send it lower; these conditions are covered in Chapter 5 in the section on shots that curve (see page 33). This chapter deals strictly with controlling the trajectory of reasonably solid shots that go reasonably straight.

How to Counterbalance Shots That Go Too Low

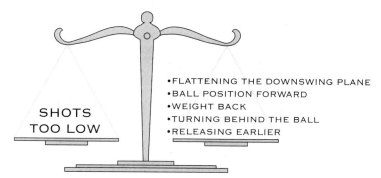

SHOTS
TOO LOW

•FLATTENING THE DOWNSWING PLANE
•BALL POSITION FORWARD
•WEIGHT BACK
•TURNING BEHIND THE BALL
•RELEASING EARLIER

FLATTENING THE DOWNSWING PLANE. This has already been covered in Chapter 5 in the section on counterbalancing pulled shots (see pages 57–59). If you make deep divots that go to the left and your shots go too low, check those corrections.

BALL POSITION FORWARD. If the ball goes too low on solid shots, one of the common causes is that the ball is positioned too far back in your stance. In a balanced swing, the bottom of the arc occurs between the left side of your face and your left armpit.

TRY THE CLUBS-ON-GROUND DRILL TO CHECK OR IMPROVE YOUR BALL POSITION (SEE PAGE 156).

WEIGHT DISTRIBUTION BACK. Sometimes the ball may be positioned correctly but you may be putting too much weight on your front (target-ward) foot.

TRY THE UPHILL-LIE DRILL TO HELP YOU FEEL A HIGHER-FLIGHT WEIGHT DISTRIBUTION (SEE PAGE 156).

TURNING BEHIND THE BALL ON THE BACKSWING. Even though you may have the ball positioned correctly and your weight distributed properly, you may be turning incorrectly, not putting enough weight behind the ball at the top of the backswing.

TRY THE SHADOW DRILL TO GET THE FEELING OF A CORRECT TURN (SEE PAGE 157).

RELEASING EARLIER. Even if you have set up correctly and gotten behind the ball correctly, you can still hit the ball too low by dragging your hands in front of it too long before releasing the clubhead.

TRY THE TEE-TO-RETEE DRILL TO DEVELOP AN EARLIER RELEASE (SEE PAGE 131).

How to Counterbalance Shots That Go Too High

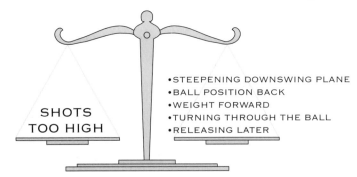

SHOTS TOO HIGH

•STEEPENING DOWNSWING PLANE
•BALL POSITION BACK
•WEIGHT FORWARD
•TURNING THROUGH THE BALL
•RELEASING LATER

STEEPENING DOWNSWING PLANE. This has already been covered in Chapter 5 in the section on counterbalancing pushed shots (see pages 60–61). If you take virtually no divot and your shots tend to start to the right and go too high, check those corrections.

BALL POSITION BACK. If the ball goes too high on solid shots, one of the common causes is that the ball is positioned too far forward in your stance. In a balanced swing, the bottom of the arc occurs between the left side of the face and the left armpit.

TRY THE CLUBS-ON-GROUND DRILL TO CHECK AND/OR IMPROVE YOUR BALL POSITION (SEE PAGE 156).

WEIGHT DISTRIBUTION FORWARD. Sometimes the ball may be positioned correctly but you may have tilted your upper body too far behind the ball.

TRY THE LEFT-SIDE-AGAINST-WALL DRILL TO ADJUST YOUR WEIGHT DISTRIBUTION (SEE PAGE 135).

TURNING THROUGH THE BALL. Even though your setup and backswing may be correct, you may be "hanging back" with your upper body on the downswing, making the ball go too high.

TRY THE SHADOW DRILL TO HELP YOU TURN THROUGH THE SHOT (SEE PAGE 157).

RELEASING LATER. Even though your body may be positioned correctly throughout the swing, you may be "casting" the clubhead down before your hands, causing the ball to go too high.

TRY THE KNOCKDOWN-UNDER-ROPE DRILL TO HELP YOU RELEASE THE CLUB LATER (SEE PAGE 158).

EIGHT

How to Balance Shots That Go the Wrong Distance

Because of relatively recent changes in modern courses, golf has become a game of power. Courses today are lush and long, placing a premium on distance. At the same time, they are heavily bunkered and the greens are fast, emphasizing a variety of short-game shots and a delicate putting touch. Tiger Woods is probably the prototypical golfer for the twenty-first century. He is tall and athletic, hits the ball incredible distances, and has good touch with his short game.

Golfers, it seems, have always wanted to hit the ball farther. But due to the recent changes in course architecture and modern watering systems, the search for added distance has become more popular than ever. Manufacturers are producing clubs and balls that have lengthened most golfers' games.

And the golfers who play professionally are taller and stronger than in previous decades. However, the fundamentals that produce distance in a golf swing really haven't changed.

An interesting phenomenon in this day of long-distance golf is that some players have actually made changes to *reduce* their distance to enhance accuracy. As a result, many of those players have done much better. Nick Faldo, Davis Love III, and Curtis Strange come to mind, as well as the aforementioned Tiger Woods with his iron game. So let's examine what produces or reduces distance.

How to Counterbalance Shots That Go Too Short

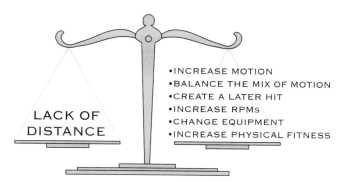

LACK OF
DISTANCE

- INCREASE MOTION
- BALANCE THE MIX OF MOTION
- CREATE A LATER HIT
- INCREASE RPMS
- CHANGE EQUIPMENT
- INCREASE PHYSICAL FITNESS

INCREASE THE AMOUNT OF MOTION. If you take a ball and roll it down a ramp, the farther up the ramp you start the ball, the farther it will go. You build up momentum. The same is true in a golf swing. The longer you swing, within the realm of good fundamentals, the more potential clubhead speed you can generate. You create motion in three ways: (1) by turning the body, (2) by swinging the arms, and (3) by cocking the wrists. If your swing is short (the clubshaft less than parallel to the ground at the top of the swing with a driver), use the following drills to lengthen your swing:

TRY THE CLUB-ACROSS-SHOULDERS DRILL FOR A BETTER TURN (SEE PAGE 158).

TRY THE WEIGHTED-CLUB DRILL FOR A LONGER ARM SWING (SEE PAGE 159).

TRY THE PRESET DRILL FOR A BETTER WRIST COCK (SEE PAGE 159).

BALANCE THE MIX OF MOTION. Not only is it important to have enough length on your swing, it is crucial to create that length with the correct *mix* of motion. The ideal mix of motion for a 5-iron: (1) a 90-degree shoulder turn, (2) a 90-degree bend in the right elbow, and (3) a 90-degree wrist cock. If you underuse one part and overuse another part on the backswing, then you have to do the same on the downswing. This only reduces power because the underused parts have to "wait" for the other parts to catch up. This waiting is not dynamic; therefore you lose distance.

TRY THE THREE-90-DEGREES DRILL FOR PROPER SHOULDER TURN, ELBOW BEND, AND WRIST COCK (SEE PAGE 160).

CREATE A LATER HIT. To maximize your power, your swing should resemble the cracking of a whip. When you crack a whip, you move the handle forward and at the last second you crack it. The sooner you start to crack it, the less power you have. The same is true in a golf swing. You should carry the handle all the way to the ball before you "crack the whip."

TRY THE CHIP-PUNCH DRILL FOR A LATER HIT (SEE PAGE 133).

INCREASE RPMS. As you swing, your body makes a small circle, the hands a larger circle, and the clubhead an even larger circle. It's like a track meet on a curved track. If all the runners start even with each other, then the outside runners have to go much faster than the inside runners to stay even. The same is true in a golf swing. For all the "runners"—that is, your body, hands, and clubhead—to reach the finish line at the same time, you have to have timing. If *all* of your "runners" go faster and still maintain this timing, you end up with a faster record—or faster clubhead speed. A lot of golfers simply swing too easy. You should strive to swing the clubhead as fast as you can while still maintaining your timing.

TRY THE SWISH DRILL FOR FASTER CLUBHEAD SPEED (SEE PAGE 161).

CHANGE EQUIPMENT. The four steps discussed above can increase your speed, given your present equipment. However, you can increase the length of your shots by making some simple changes in that equipment. The longest ball is the one that spins the least, and most two-piece balls spin less than wound ones. The longer the clubshaft, the more speed you can create; the new, lighter-weight heads on modern clubs make this a feasible alternative. You might give up some accuracy, however. Generally, the less loft a club has, the farther the ball will go. The adjusted weighting (toward the sole) on many of the new clubs allows the ball to still go a normal height even when the loft is lower. Check with your golf professional when you make these changes so you can get the correct fit for your game.

INCREASE PHYSICAL FITNESS. A car that is beautifully manufactured still won't go very fast if the engine is deficient in horsepower. The same is true in a golf swing. Anything you can do to increase your strength, flexibility, and quickness will aid you in hitting the ball farther. There are a number of qualified trainers in this field and a number of good books on golf fitness, such as the one from the Centinela Hospital.

TRY THE WEIGHTED-CLUB DRILL TO INCREASE THE STRENGTH OF YOUR GOLF MUSCLES (SEE PAGE 159).

How to Counterbalance Shots That Go Too Far

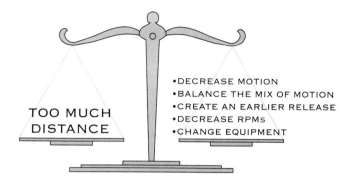

TOO MUCH DISTANCE

- DECREASE MOTION
- BALANCE THE MIX OF MOTION
- CREATE AN EARLIER RELEASE
- DECREASE RPMs
- CHANGE EQUIPMENT

You may think hitting the ball too far is not a problem. However, controlling distance is one of the most important aspects of shooting low scores. A number of golfers have a hard time controlling their distance, especially on approach shots, because they have *too much* clubhead speed. In addition, an effective short game (pitches and chips) revolves around distance control. A lot of the drills here will be related to the short game.

DECREASE THE AMOUNT OF MOTION. Sometimes you can create too much motion on the backswing. Then you must actually slow down on the downswing to hit the ball the right distance. You can see this a lot in the short game. A player takes the club back too far and has to decelerate coming down. Regarding the full swing, look at John Daly's method. His swing is so long he creates a lot of distance, but he's always at the bottom of the tour statistics for accuracy. Strive for the clubshaft to be parallel with the ground at the top of the backswing with the driver, but stay short of that with the other clubs.

TRY THE THREE-90-DEGREES DRILL TO IMPROVE YOUR LONG-GAME DISTANCE CONTROL (SEE PAGE 160).

TRY THE VARIABLE-BACKSWING DRILL TO IMPROVE YOUR SHORT-GAME DISTANCE CONTROL (SEE PAGE 162).

BALANCE THE MIX OF MOTION. Sometimes you achieve the right amount of motion but get out of balance with the mix of motion. To reduce distance, reduce all of the parts proportionally—your shoulder turn, bend in right elbow, and wrist cock. This is the easiest way to control distance.

Reducing any part of the motion, however, will also tend to reduce distance.

TRY THE FIRM-IT-UP DRILL TO IMPROVE YOUR MIX-OF-MOTION BALANCE (SEE PAGE 163).

CREATE AN EARLIER RELEASE. Just as a late hit will create more distance, an earlier release will create less distance. Have the feeling that the clubhead is coming down in a wide arc rather than a narrow one.

TRY THE 1-INCH, 2-INCH, 3-INCH DRILL FOR AN EARLIER RELEASE (SEE PAGE 163).

DECREASE RPMS. Simply swing slower to hit shorter. Sometimes golfers just swing too hard and fast. Learning to control your swing speed is a critical factor.

TRY THE FULL-SWING, VARIABLE-DISTANCE DRILL TO BETTER CONTROL YOUR CLUBHEAD SPEED (SEE PAGE 164).

CHANGE EQUIPMENT. Just as most equipment is designed to hit the ball longer, some equipment is designed to hit the ball shorter. Balls that spin more tend to go shorter, and most wound balls spin more than conventional two-piece balls. Clubs that spin the ball more tend to make it go shorter— for instance, irons with different grooves. For most players, more loft also makes the ball go shorter (you might prefer a 10-degree driver rather than an 8-degree one, for example). A lot of Tour professionals today carry at least three wedges to hit the shorter shots. The higher-lofted wedges allow you to make a fuller swing without fear that the ball will go too far. Finally, shorter shafts make the ball go shorter. Again, see your golf professional to fit your needs correctly.

Balancing Your

Short Game

A man who can chip and putt is a match for anyone.
A man who can't is a match for no one.
—HARVEY PENICK

This is a special chapter on the short game. I've included it in this book for three reasons. First, this part of the game is extremely important. For the average player, putts, chips, pitches, and bunker shots make up some 75 percent of all shots played in a round. Second, even though the fundamentals listed in the earlier chapters apply to the short game as well, we are conditioned to think of the short game as a separate part of golf. But it isn't. Faults that appear in your full swing often are present in your part swings, too. Third, there *are* different emphases that need to be applied to a balanced short game. So let's begin.

GETTING YOUR PUTTING IN BALANCE

When it comes to putting, you have several different factors to consider. First, putting is the only part of the game where the equipment and the technique are designed to *roll* the ball along the ground throughout the shot. Second, creating a lot of distance is not necessary in putting. Finally, putting requires less athletic ability and more precision than any other part of the game.

Putting is best presented in this order: (1) technique for a sound and balanced putting stroke (direction, distance, trajectory and spin; (2) a balanced approach to reading greens; and (3) a balanced putting strategy.

Technique for a Sound and Balanced Putting Stroke

THE COMPLETED PUTTING GRIP, WITH PALMS FACING EACH OTHER.

DIRECTION. The direction of a putt is controlled by the same two factors that control the direction of all shots: the direction the club*face* is looking at the moment of impact and the *path* the clubhead is traveling at impact. Of the two, the direction of the clubface is at least twice as important as the path the clubhead swings along. Why? Because the slower the club is moving on any shot, the more the flight of the ball is influenced by the clubface. As the speed of the club increases, so does the influence of the path of the swing. Obviously, in putting, the club moves slower than on any other shot.

The clubface. As in all other shots, the two main factors in controlling the clubface are the grip you use and the wrist position at impact. Knowing this, I advocate a completely different grip for putting than for shots calling for more distance. I recommend two main changes: (1) position the grip in the lifelines of both hands, as opposed to in the fingers, and (2) position both palms so they face each other or face *skyward* to the same degree. As Harvey Penick said, "They make putter grips flat on top for a reason . . . that's where your thumbs go." The more the palms face skyward (equally), the squarer the clubface will remain. However, this positioning tends to reduce feel, at least initially.

The reason I recommend this grip is because it tends to lock the wrists. The only purpose of wrist action in any golf swing is to produce speed. In putting, you don't need to create speed. Also, if you eliminate wrist action in putting, then the face of the putter can stay square to the path on which it swings, eliminating manipulation.

FIND THE SWEET SPOT WITH A PENCIL ERASER . . . . . . THEN MARK IT WITH THE PENCIL.

Clubhead path. There is a lot of confusion about the most efficient path for the swinging of the putter. Some players and teachers advocate a straight-back, straight-through stroke, while others suggest an inside-to-on-the-line-to-back-inside arc to the stroke. My feeling is that just like all of the other clubs, the putter swings along a *plane* dictated by the lie of the putter. The more upright the putter, the more straight back and through the stroke appears. The flatter the putter, the more inside to inside the path appears—the same way a wedge swing looks upright, while a driver swing looks flat.

TRY THE PLANE-BOARD DRILL TO GET THE FEELING OF AN "ON PLANE" STROKE (SEE PAGE 165).

DISTANCE. The distance a putt travels is governed by two things: (1) solidness of contact and (2) clubhead speed.

Solidness of contact. The sweet spot is not always in the center of the putter face. To determine the sweet spot on your putter, use the following procedure: Hold the putter lightly with your thumb and first finger at the grip end. Tap the face with the eraser end of a pencil until you find the point on the putter face at which there is no twist or vibration. That's the sweet spot. Mark it with the pencil.

TRY THE BAND-AID DRILL TO LEARN TO HIT THE BALL CONSISTENTLY ON THE SWEET SPOT (SEE PAGE 166).

Clubhead speed. Most great putters have used only one power source for putting. Billy Casper, Ben Hogan,

A BALANCED PUTTING STROKE . . .   . . . IS THE SAME GOING BACK . . .   . . . AS COMING THROUGH.

and Bob Rosburg locked the body and arms and used only the wrists to create power. Arnold Palmer locked his body and wrists and used just his arms. Most of the modern players (Tom Watson in his prime, Phil Mickelson, and Ben Crenshaw) keep their arms and wrists at a fixed angle and move the putter with their shoulders. This evolution was due to the increasing speed of the greens on the Tour. Bigger body muscles are slow-moving, while arm and wrist muscles are quick. The main message I want you to have, however, is to use only one power source for putting. If you don't already putt with one power source, I recommend fixing the arms and wrists and using just the shoulders.

Just as great putters have used different power sources, they have used different speeds as the ball hits the hole. Palmer, Watson, Paul Azinger, and John Daly "charge" the ball at the hole. If they miss the putt, the ball tends to go 2 to 3 feet past the hole. There are advantages to putting this way: (1) the ball always gets to the hole, (2) it holds the line better on bumpy greens, and (3) you can play less break. But there are disadvantages: (1) you're faced with a lot of "nervous" second putts, and (2) the usable size of the hole is smaller. Other great putters such as Lee Trevino, Ben Crenshaw, and Phil Mickelson tend to "die" the ball at the hole. The advantages to this type of speed are that you rarely have a long second putt and the usable size of the

"A good stroke stays low to the ground, but I don't like a student trying to do that."
—HARVEY PENICK

hole is larger—the ball will fall in from the edges of the hole. The disadvantages are that the ball is moved off line easier by imperfections on the green, and if you mis-hit the putt at all, the ball will not reach the hole.

There is an ideal speed when the ball reaches the hole, however, that has been determined by research. That speed would carry a missed putt about 20 inches past the hole. This was determined by hitting putts that would go at the slowest possible speed to reach the hole and by hitting putts that would move at the maximum speed and still go in the hole. By varying the speed between these two extremes, it was found that the ideal speed that would carry through imperfections and still have gravity to put the ball in the hole would roll the ball 20 inches past.*

What often creates a certain speed of putting is grip pressure. Those who charge putts tend to grip firmly, while those who die putts tend to grip lightly. However, one of the greatest indications of good putting is that there is very little, if any, change in pressure throughout the stroke. Changing grip pressure throughout the stroke causes both distance and direction problems. **TRY THE TEE-TO-TEE DRILL, THE CLOSED-EYES DRILL, THE ROLL-BALL-OFF-RAMP DRILL TO DEVELOP A FEEL FOR DISTANCE (SEE PAGES 167 AND 168).**

TRAJECTORY AND SPIN. You may think this section is unnecessary. All putts roll on the ground, so there is only one trajectory, right? Wrong. I've found that only with the top putters, putting their best, does the ball stay on the ground. To some degree, most amateurs I've seen fly their putts in the air with backspin.

The technique I used to discover these facts came from Carl Welty, a teaching professional at La Costa in Carlsbad, California. Carl had a large number of participants in the Tournament of Champions field putt balls with a stripe on them. He started the stripe horizontal to the ground. Then, using a high-speed camera, he noticed that on a putt of about 30 feet, most of the putts would skid for two frames and then start rolling.

I started filming my students and noticed that most amateurs actually hit the putt with loft, causing it to fly for a while with the stripe backing up. But when I filmed Ben Crenshaw, his ball had turned down half a revolution on the first frame. There are two reasons for this: First, almost all putters are made with built-in loft to some degree, and most amateurs' hands are even with or behind the ball at impact, allowing loft and backspin to be

*From *The Golf Shot* by Michael Biddulph (New York: W. W. Norton, 1980).

> "I'm not a believer in never up, never in. If there's any break at all, that ball will have sidespin, and it can't stay in the hole if it's moving too fast. It's better to give luck a chance."
> —HARVEY PENICK

imparted to the shot. But Crenshaw's hands are in front of the putter head, reducing the loft to 0 degrees. Second, this also allows impact to be higher on the ball, creating little or no backspin. The ball skids less and starts rolling sooner.

TRY THE UNDER-SHAFT DRILL FOR LOW BACKSWING AND SMOOTHER ROLL (SEE PAGE 169).

A Balanced Approach to Reading Greens

What are the two most important aspects of green-reading? First, consistent ball speed, and second, the player's experience. Before you can expect to read greens well, your ball needs to be traveling toward the hole at a consistent speed. If you charge one putt and then die another, your mind will never assimilate the right information to know how much break to play. Every time you have a putt, your mind takes a picture of it. You then subconsciously notice where you aim and where the putt goes. The next time you have a similar putt, your mind can start to make adjustments based on this past experience. The more pictures you have in your mind, the more precise the adjustments. That's why I'm not a big believer in keeping your eyes looking down after impact and listening for the putt to fall. That technique makes your pictures incomplete.

There are three factors you must consider when reading a putt: (1) the speed of the green, (2) the slope of the green, and (3) the grain of the green.

THE SPEED OF THE GREEN. The easiest way to get a feel for the speed of the green is to go to the practice green before you play and hit different types of putts. If the ball goes shorter than you expect, obviously the greens are slow to you. So remember the ball will not break as much and you need to play a straighter line. If the ball goes longer than you expect, then the greens are fast to you and you will need to allow for more break than you normally would.

TRY THE 2-FEET-PAST DRILL AND THE TEE-AROUND-HOLE DRILL TO LEARN GREEN SPEED (SEE PAGES 169 AND 170).

THE SLOPE OF THE GREEN. There are two types of slopes on a green. First, there is the general slope of the green and the terrain around it. This general slope is affected by the high and low points of the property and the way water drains off the green. If a course is built in hilly terrain, the general slope will be away from the highest points and toward the valleys. Just imagine how water would flow off the green if you poured a huge bucket onto the putting surface. Second, there are the special mounds and terraces built into the green by the architect. Both types of slopes have to be judged when reading a green, and experience is the only way to master them.

THE GRAIN OF THE GREEN. On most courses today, grain (or the direction the grass grows) is not as much a factor as in the past. Why? The blades of grass in the modern strains are so much narrower and cut so much shorter that they won't affect a ball as much as the older, coarser grasses did. But there is still some effect from grain. If you live in the South, where the grasses must thrive in the sun and may not require a lot of water, you have to factor in grain. Sun-seeking grasses grow toward the setting sun. In the North, you need grasses that require more watering. Water-seeking grasses grow downhill.

Generally, grass that looks shiny or light in color is with the grain and the putt will be faster. Grass that looks darker is against the grain and the putt will be slower. Your greens may contain a checkerboard effect in the morning, which means that the grass is lying in the direction in which the mower mowed it. But unless you play on older, coarser Bermuda greens in the South, grain should not be much of a factor.

PUTTS WILL BREAK IN THE SAME DIRECTION WATER WOULD FLOW.

"I like to see that putt die out straight."
—HARVEY PENICK

A Balanced Putting Strategy

There is a distinct mindset to putting that determines strategy. The best way to imagine this strategy is to remember the colors of a stoplight: green, yellow, and red.

Green means go for it! This would be for putts of 12 feet or less. Your mindset should be to hole the putt. Your main attention should be on the line of the putt because you will rarely misread the speed from that distance.

In the stroke itself, a player who overaccelerates (follow-through longer than the backswing) is generally a good green-zone putter. I don't recommend making a change in your stroke for any putt, but you must guard against decelerating in the green zone.

Yellow means go with caution. This would be for putts of 12 feet to 25 feet. Your mindset is still to hole the putt, but to do so with an attitude that if you miss the putt, your second putt will be an easy one. As you stroke the putt, you should give equal attention to line and speed.

Red means stop thinking about holing the putt and concentrate instead on trying to take no more than two putts. You should have a defensive posture on putts of more than 25 feet. You should be concerned mainly with the speed of the putt and only generally regard the line, since most three-putts come from poor distance control.

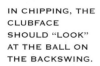

"Most players hit the ball too high around the green, or take too much loft."

—HARVEY PENICK

GETTING YOUR CHIPPING IN BALANCE

IN CHIPPING, THE CLUBFACE SHOULD "LOOK" AT THE BALL ON THE BACKSWING.

I consider a chip to be a low, rolling shot that flies no farther than one-third the total distance of the shot. Any short-game shot that flies farther would be considered a pitch in this book. To balance out your chipping technique, we will talk about the factors that control a chip shot: (1) direction, (2) distance, (3) trajectory, and (4) a balanced chipping strategy.

Direction

Just as in all shots, there are two factors that control direction: (1) the clubface alignment at impact and (2) the clubhead path at impact.

THE CLUBFACE ALIGNMENT AT IMPACT. Obviously, at impact you want the clubface to "look" in the direction you want to send the ball. However, I have found that the best way to do this is to keep the clubface looking at the *ball* throughout the backswing and looking at the *target* through impact. This "hooded" action creates consistency. Usually, this shot is not long, and when you make a short swing, it is too difficult to time a lot of opening and closing of the clubface (see photo).

THE CLUBHEAD PATH AT IMPACT. I think the club should swing on the plane that is dictated by the lie of the club you are using. But if you don't swing the club along that plane, you are much better off swinging on a steeper or more outside path as opposed to having the club swing inside the target line.

Distance

The distance of the shot comes from two factors: (1) the effective loft of the club at impact, (2) the speed of the clubhead at impact, and (3) the use of a single lever and two levers.

THE EFFECTIVE LOFT OF THE CLUB AT IMPACT. Obviously, the less loft a club has at impact, the farther the ball will go, given the same clubhead speed. You can change the loft of a shot in two ways: (1) club selection and (2) ball position. You can make a ball go lower (and farther) or higher (and shorter) just by choosing a club with less or more loft. My friend Paul Runyan, the two-time PGA champion, uses all of the irons in his bag to chip. A recent trend even calls for using fairway woods! Quite obviously, Paul might select a 2-iron when he wants the ball to go a very short distance in the air and a long distance on the ground. To the contrary, he would pick a wedge when he wants the ball to fly higher and roll less.

I believe in a little different system for most people. Since most chip shots are not hit very hard, any mistake hitting behind the ball is quite penal: the club is slowed dramatically by the turf. Therefore, to avoid the "turf first" shot, I recommend playing the chip toward the back of the stance, which produces a steeper angle of approach, helping to hit the ball before the ground. This ball-back position puts the handle of the club farther in front of the clubhead, reducing the effective loft of the club. Therefore, a 9-iron might have the loft of a 7-iron, and a 7-iron might have the loft of a 5-iron, and so forth. These are considerations you have to take into account when planning on the flight of the ball (see photos).

TOP:
THE BASIC CHIPPING SETUP: BALL BACK, HANDS AND WEIGHT AHEAD.

BOTTOM:
LETTING THE CLUB SWING FROM HIGH TO LOW THROUGH IMPACT CAUSES THE BALL TO BECOME AIRBORNE. THERE IS NO NEED TO LIFT THE CLUB INTO THE AIR ON THE THROUGH SWING.

FOR SHORTER CHIPS: A SINGLE-LEVER GRIP PROMOTES CONSISTENT CONTACT.

FOR LONGER CHIPS: A NORMAL GRIP GENERATES MORE CLUBHEAD SPEED.

THE SPEED OF THE CLUBHEAD AT IMPACT. The second factor that determines the distance a chip shot goes is the speed of the clubhead at impact. The greater the clubhead speed, the more loft you need to chip the ball a given distance.

THE USE OF A SINGLE LEVER AND TWO LEVERS. In the balanced putting stroke, we control the distance by eliminating all the hinging—or leverage—of the wrists. You can do the same for chipping. By using your putting grip and stroke, you can control short chips much more easily with just one lever. However, as more distance is required, you will need more power. This is best accomplished by changing to your full-swing grip and allowing for some wrist cock—and extra leverage—to create clubhead speed without a lot more effort (see photos).

Trajectory

Controlling trajectory and spin is really what determines a number of things in chipping. Deciding on your trajectory determines your (1) club selection, (2) ball position, and (3) weight distribution.

CLUB SELECTION. Obviously, the less loft a club has, the lower and longer the shot, all other things being equal. I think most golfers probably use too much loft in their club selection. However, if you use the ball-back theory of chipping (as previously mentioned), you must select a club with enough loft to be able to *deloft* it to create the preferred downward angle of approach.

BALL POSITION. Since the bottom of the swing occurs in a "flat spot" area running from under the left side of your face to your left armpit, the ball can be placed anywhere from the left armpit back toward the right foot. Any ball played forward of the left armpit will be hit on the upswing, causing you to top the ball. Anything played in the flat spot will be hit with a sweeping blow and anything behind the flat spot will be hit on the downswing. The farther back you position the ball in the stance, the lower the shot; the farther forward you position it, the higher the shot.

WEIGHT DISTRIBUTION. Your weight can be distributed equally on both feet, more on the left foot, or more on the right foot. The more weight you put on your left foot, the lower the ball tends to go; and the more weight you put on your right foot, the higher the ball tends to go. The reason you might adjust your weight instead of just relying on ball position to influence the trajectory of your shot is that changing your weight influences your angle of steepness more than just ball position does. The more weight you put on your left foot, the more high to low the clubhead travels through impact; the more weight you put on your right foot, the more low to high it travels.

A Balanced Chipping Strategy

Dick Aultman, a former Golf Digest Schools instructor, gave me the best way to remember your strategy around the greens. Just keep in mind the initials LTD: L means *lie,* T means *trajectory,* and D means *distance.*

BALL POSITION FOR HIGH GRASS.   BARE GROUND.   BALL SITTING UP.

LIE. The lie of the ball tells you what you can do with the shot. If the ball is sitting in a bad lie (deep in grass or on bare ground), you must hit down because there is no room under the ball to sweep it. As the lie improves (meaning more air or cushion under the ball), the more forward your ball position *can* be and the more level the angle of approach *could* be. However, that doesn't mean you must sweep the ball more on a good lie, only that you have the option (see photos).

TRAJECTORY. My suggestion to you is to visualize landing the ball about three feet on the green, picking the trajectory that will allow the ball to roll the rest of the way. This is the safest, most predictable option because it requires the least amount of clubhead speed for the shot.

DISTANCE. The length of the shot determines whether you use your putting grip and a no-wrist stroke (single lever) or your full-swing grip and a two-lever stroke. Longer shots require a two-lever stroke.

PICKING THE RIGHT CLUB. The order for short-game club selection: (1) putt whenever it is possible, (2) chip with the least loft possible, and (3) use the least motion possible. *Note:* If you are just learning the game, I would recommend a different philosophy. At first, use just your pitching wedge from anywhere around the green. After you are able to use this club acceptably, then begin to add other clubs to your short-game arsenal.

Chuck Cook: "Harvey, why didn't you change Cindy's [Figg-Currier's] grip in college? Why did you wait until she turned pro?" Harvey Penick: "Because her short game wasn't good enough."

GETTING YOUR PITCHING IN BALANCE

I consider a pitch to be any short-game shot that flies more than one-third of the total distance of the shot. To balance out your pitching technique, we will look at the same factors we considered in chipping: (1) direction, (2) distance, (3) trajectory, and (4) a balanced pitching strategy.

Direction

Just as in all shots, the two factors that control direction are (1) the clubface alignment at impact and (2) the clubhead path at impact.

THE CLUBFACE ALIGNMENT AT IMPACT. In pitch shots designed to go high, the clubface must be either square to the path of the swing or open to that path. You set up at address by squaring or opening the face as much as needed. Therefore, you have a different priority in the pitch-shot swing than

PICK CLUB AND TRAJECTORY THAT WILL ALLOW YOU TO LAND THE BALL ON THE GREEN AND ABOUT ONE-THIRD OF THE WAY TO THE HOLE.

in the chip-shot swing. In the chip shot, we wanted the clubface square (or "hooded") on the backswing. On the pitch shot, we want the clubface to be in a "toe up" position halfway back (see photo). Trying to hit a high shot from a "hooded" position leads to scooping.

THE CLUBHEAD PATH AT IMPACT. The path of the swing must match the position of the clubface. If the clubface is square, you must aim and swing on a plane that is parallel to the target line. If you open the face, you must align your body to the left and swing on a plane that is parallel to your leftward body alignment. The biggest mistake people make when pitching is to swing too much inside to out in relation to their body alignment. This produces fat, thin, and shanked shots, as well as poor distance control.

IN PITCHING, THE TOE OF THE CLUB SHOULD POINT TOWARD THE SKY HALFWAY BACK.

Distance

The distance of the pitch shot is determined by two factors: (1) the effective loft of the club at impact and (2) the speed of the club at impact. In chip-

A NORMAL PITCHING SETUP: BALL UNDER THE LEFT SIDE OF YOUR FACE, WEIGHT EVENLY DISTRIBUTED, CLUBFACE SQUARE.

SETUP FOR A HIGH PITCH.

SETUP FOR A LOW PITCH.

PERFECTLY BALANCED GOLF

ping, more often than not you reduce the effective loft of a club to hit the lower shots. In pitching, you tend to increase the effective loft of a club by opening the face or positioning the ball more forward in the stance, or both (see photos). Speed is still created in one of two ways: a single-lever (firm wrists) stroke or a double-lever (wrists cocking) stroke. On some very delicate short pitches, you may want to use a single-lever stroke, but because you are using more loft for pitching, in general you will use your full-swing grip and wrist action for most pitch shots.

Trajectory

Your trajectory is also influenced by the same three factors as in chipping: (1) club selection, (2) ball position, and (3) weight distribution. I would encourage you to use only your *sand wedge* and your *lob wedges* for pitch shots. There are several reasons for this: (a) the loft of the club is built in and needs no help; (b) there is more weight on the bottom of the club, aiding higher shots; and (c) the bottom of the club is designed to skid and not dig, giving you a larger margin of error from most lies. (The flange on a sand or lob wedge is designed so the leading edge is higher than the trailing edge, creating "bounce." If the sole of the club contacts the ground slightly behind the ball, the club will still slide under the ball instead of digging into the ground.) Again, the farther back you position the ball in your stance, the lower the shot will be. On most pitch shots, you normally need more swing to make up for the added loft of the shot. Therefore, you will have some weight shift with the shot, both back and through. However, for a low pitch, you can position your weight more to the left; and for a high pitch, more to the right (see photos).

Note: You have a range of ingredients to mix in the short game. Use them as your counterbalances:

Very low shots = low-lofted clubs + ball back + weight left.

Very high shots = high-lofted clubs with the face open + ball forward + weight right.

And everything in between.

A Balanced Pitching Strategy

The late Davis Love, Jr., once gave me a great strategy for shots around the green. He said you have four ways to stop the ball, and this is the order in which to use them: (1) lack of inertia: this happens with putting—you hit the ball a certain speed and then it runs out of steam and stops; (2) trajectory: you hit the ball a certain height and it stops due to lack of roll; (3) spin: you create backspin to stop the ball (unpredictable); and (4) friction: you run the ball through grass around the green, slowing the ball down (more unpredictable).

Paul Runyan also gave me a credo I use for deciding how to play shots around the green. He says you have two usable strokes: (1) you hit down on the ball (pinch), and (2) you sweep the ball. You also have two clubface positions: (1) square and (2) open (to varying degrees). He uses this order of choosing his strokes: first, hit down with a square face; second, hit down with an open face; third, sweep with a square face; and fourth, sweep with an open face.

TRY THE PAINT-A-FACE-ON-THE-FACE DRILL TO MAINTAIN LOFT (SEE PAGE 172).

A BALANCED WAY TO PLAY BUNKERS

The greenside bunker shot is dramatically different from any other shot in golf. Essentially, this is because the club doesn't contact the ball. Rather, it contacts the sand underneath it. We will discuss (1) technique, (2) use of the flange, (3) controlling distance, and (4) different lies.

Technique

Most teachers say that in the bunker your primary goal should be to hit behind the ball. I would rather you not think in those terms. I recommend you simply swing the clubhead *lower* than the ball, taking the sand *underneath* the ball out of the bunker and onto the green. The ball will ride out on this cushion of sand.

Obviously, if you swing underneath the ball, you *will* hit behind the ball. However, most students I see who try to hit behind the ball hit too far behind it. Therefore, they hit the shot "fat" just as they would on grass if they aimed behind the ball. So I recommend that you look *at* the ball and try to swing lower than the ball.

TRY THE TEE-IN-THE-BUNKER DRILL TO LEARN PROPER TECHNIQUE OUT OF SAND (SEE PAGE 173).

You want the sand wedge to be underneath the ball while the club is traveling in the "flat spot" of the swing. Therefore, you should position the ball directly under the left side of your face, between your left cheek and your left armpit.

Use of the Flange

The sand wedge is designed differently from the other irons in that the trailing edge of its sole—or the flange—is lower than the leading edge (see photo). In most other irons, the trailing edge is even with the leading edge (in other words, the bottom of the club is flat). This unique design of the flange is called the "bounce" of the club. I would rather you labeled the two edges of the flange differently, however. I would prefer you label the trailing edge the "skidding" edge and the leading edge the "digging" edge. This labeling actually tells you when to use each edge as you play different shots.

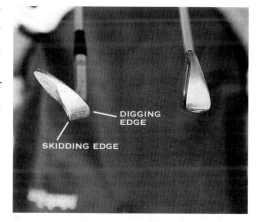

Use the skidding edge anytime you have a good lie in the sand. Why? When the club enters the sand with the skidding edge, the club first goes underneath the ball and then skids along the divot, making the divot hole very level, and then comes out on the front side of the ball. Employing this skidding edge keeps the club from digging too much into the sand. To use this edge, you should address the ball with your hands in the center of your body (see photo). This hands-behind-the-ball setup encourages the skidding edge to hit the sand first.

If you have a bad lie (buried under the sand), or if the sand is wet and compact, you should use the digging edge of the sand wedge. If this front edge of the club hits the sand first, the club will continue to dig deeper into the sand. To play a buried lie, set up as if you had a good lie and then sim-

NOT ONLY DOES THE BOUNCE ON A SAND WEDGE (LEFT) ALLOW THE CLUB TO SLIDE THROUGH THE GRASS, MAKING IT A BETTER CLUB FOR MOST PITCH SHOTS, IT IS ALSO THE PREFERRED CLUB IN THE SAND. THE SKIDDING EDGE AND THE DIGGING EDGE GIVE THE CLUB EXTREME VERSATILITY.

NORMAL BUNKER SETUP: USING THE
SKIDDING EDGE.

USING THE DIGGING EDGE.

ply put your weight toward the target, allowing your hands to position themselves in front of the ball (see photo). When hitting the shot, don't try to follow through. Just allow the club to keep digging into the sand underneath the ball, "popping" it out of the bunker. Try to allow for more roll than normal.

TRY THE SAND-THE-FLANGE DRILL TO LEARN PROPER SAND DISPLACEMENT (SEE PAGE 174).

Controlling Distance

It is dangerous to use too little clubhead speed in the bunker: you need enough speed to carry out not only the ball but also the cushion of sand un-

SQUARE CLUBFACE FOR A
LONGER EXPLOSION SHOT.

OPEN A LITTLE FOR A MEDIUM
SHOT.

OPEN A LOT FOR A SHORT SHOT.

PERFECTLY BALANCED GOLF

1. "DIAL" THE CLUBFACE . . .

2. TAKE YOUR GRIP . . .

3. WALK AROUND THE BALL TO THE
LEFT . . .

4. SWING ON A PLANE THAT PARALLELS
YOUR BODY LINE.

derneath it. A good way to control the distance of the shot is by how much loft you put on the sand wedge. You can either open the clubface or square it. The more you open the clubface, the higher—and shorter—the shot will go. The more you square the clubface, the lower—and longer—the shot will go. When the clubface is square, the stance should be square or parallel to the target line. As you open the clubface to reduce the distance of the shot, and to increase the height of the shot, open your stance a corresponding amount. Think of the clubface as a dial. You can "dial" the clubface open the amount you need, then take your grip. Finally, walk around the ball to the left until the clubface is almost looking at the target. Then swing on a plane that parallels your body line. This will make the ball go at your target, and it will go the correct distance. (See photos.)

Different Lies

This is the part of bunker play that is quite challenging, but a lot of fun. The following shots are not so hard if you make some simple adjustments to balance out their tendencies.

AN UPHILL LIE REQUIRES SHOULDERS PARALLEL WITH THE SLOPE . . .

. . . THEN A FOLLOW-THROUGH ALONG THE SLOPE LINE.

PERFECTLY BALANCED GOLF

A DOWNHILL LIE ALSO REQUIRES
SHOULDERS PARALLEL WITH THE
SLOPE.

HARD SAND.

SOFT SAND.

UPHILL LIES. When your ball is lying on an uphill slope in the bunker, it will go shorter. Balance this out by simply aligning your shoulders parallel to the slope and using a squarer clubface than you normally would for a shot of the same length from a level lie.

DOWNHILL LIES. When your ball is lying on a downhill slope, it will go farther. Counterbalance this by simply aligning your body parallel to the slope and using a more open clubface than you normally would for a shot of the same length from a level lie.

HARD SAND. When your ball is on hard-packed sand, it will go farther than normal. Therefore, counterbalance that by opening the clubface more than you would for a shot of the same distance from a normal texture of sand. Since the sand is harder to penetrate, however, counterbalance that by also putting your weight and hands forward to allow the skidding edge to penetrate.

FOR A VERY LONG EXPLOSION, USE AN
8- OR 9-IRON, OPEN THE FACE . . .

. . . AND MAKE YOUR NORMAL BUNKER
SWING.

SOFT SAND. If the sand is unusually soft and fluffy, the ball will go shorter than normal because the club tends to dig more. Counterbalance that by playing with a squarer clubface than normal and moving the ball slightly more forward to level out the bottom of your swing.

EXTRALONG GREENSIDE BUNKER SHOTS. Many golfers think these are the most difficult shots in the game. But they don't have to be. First of all, forget using your sand wedge. The counterbalance here is to use your pitching wedge, 9-iron, or even 8-iron. Just open up the clubface so you add a skidding edge to the flange. Then swing as if you were playing a normal-length sand shot with your sand wedge. This technique takes a bit of practice and lots of confidence, but it works!

SWING SEQUENCES

It has been a tremendously interesting and satisfying experience to work with Tom Kite, Payne Stewart, and Corey Pavin, three U.S. Open champions. They all have different physical builds, personalities, and swing techniques.

As we study their styles, notice that the differences are created by the different grips, which cause different clubface positions. Note that Tom Kite has a neutral grip and square clubface, which allow his body to rotate into the shot with his arms in a side-by-side position.

Payne Stewart has a strong right-hand grip, which closes the clubface. To counteract the closed face, Payne's right side slides laterally to drop his arms into an "underhanded" position through impact, counterbalancing the closed face.

Corey Pavin has a weak grip, which opens the clubface. To counteract the open face, Corey's right side "hangs back," allowing his arms to rotate over.

All three of these great champions have won the U.S. Open as well as numerous other titles. Which way is right? Their way for them, your way for you.

1. IDEAL BALANCED SETUP AND GRIP.

2. LOTS OF SHOULDER TURN, NOT MUCH
HIP TURN YET. VERY POWERFUL.

3. IDEAL. CLUBFACE SQUARE, PERFECT
LENGTH OF SWING.

4. RIGHT ARM AND WRIST REMAIN
COCKED AS UPPER BODY UNWINDS. THE
KEY TO DISTANCE!

5. LEFT WRIST FLAT, RIGHT WRIST COCKED. RIGHT ARM SOFT, BODY ROTATED.

6. NO FLIP OF THE WRISTS YET AS BOTH ARMS BECOME STRAIGHT. LEFT LEG TALL DUE TO HIPS TURNING.

7. HANDS AND ARMS IN FRONT OF BODY IN SIDE-BY-SIDE POSITION.

8. RIGHT SIDE PASSES LEFT INTO STRAIGHT BALANCED POSITION.

1. STRONG RIGHT-HAND GRIP WILL
CLOSE CLUB ON TAKEAWAY. SQUARE
LEFT FOOT LEADS TO SLIDING ON
DOWNSWING. OPEN RIGHT FOOT
ENHANCES TURN ON BACKSWING.

2. PAYNE'S TAKEAWAY IS VERY WIDE, DUE
TO LATE SETTING OF WRISTS AND ARMS.

3. TURN IS ALREADY PAST 90 DEGREES,
WRISTS JUST STARTING TO COCK.

4. BIG SWING. LOTS OF TURN, ARM
SWING, AND WRIST COCK. LEFT HEEL
OFF GROUND.

5. ARMS AND WRISTS REMAIN COCKED AS HIPS SLIDE TOWARD TARGET.

6. DUE TO CLOSED CLUBFACE, SWING IS "UNDERHANDED." HIPS MOVE LATERALLY TO DROP CLUB INTO THIS POSITION.

7. RIGHT SIDE REALLY BEGINNING TO ROTATE. NOTICE LEFT FOOT TWISTED INTO OPEN POSITION.

8. "FREE-FLOWING, GRACEFUL, AND FULL." THIS PICTURE EPITOMIZES THAT DESCRIPTION.

1. VERY WEAK GRIP, UNUSUAL COCK OF HEAD ARE ONLY VARIATIONS TO PERFECT SETUP.

2. WEAK GRIP ENCOURAGES EARLY SETTING OF WRISTS. LOTS OF TURN EARLY.

3. WEAK GRIP CAUSES OPEN CLUBFACE. RIGHT ARM A LITTLE HIGH HERE. OTHERWISE TEXTBOOK.

4. ARMS "RECONNECT" BEAUTIFULLY. LEFT WRIST BOWS TRYING TO CLOSE OPEN CLUBFACE.

5. RIGHT SIDE "HANGS BACK," ALLOWING HANDS AND ARMS TO SQUARE CLUBFACE.

6. "OVERHANDED" RELEASE GOES WITH WEAK GRIP.

7. RIGHT SIDE JUST STARTING TO RELEASE. NOTICE CROSSOVER OF ARMS.

8. RIGHT SIDE FINALLY CATCHES LEFT SIDE. FINISH LOW, DUE TO ROLLING OF ARMS.

TEN

How to Create
Off-Balance Shots
from Trouble

MEDIUM

LOW

HIGH

YOUR SETUP
GREATLY
AFFECTS THE
TRAJECTORY OF
YOUR SHOTS.

For most of this book, I have been telling you how to balance out your swing and how to play shots in balance. There are times, however, when you want to create shots that are *out of balance.* This is when you are playing from trouble, or from unusual lies or uneven stances. In this chapter, I will show you how to play (1) under trouble, (2) over trouble, (3) around trouble, and (4) from funny lies.

FOR A LOW SHOT, POSITION THE BALL BACK IN YOUR STANCE . . .

. . . AND FINISH LOW . . .

. . . TO SEND THE BALL LOW UNDER TROUBLE.

Under Trouble

There are situations on the course that call for you to hit the ball abnormally low. This might be when you have to go under a tree or into a strong wind. The best way to think of controlling the trajectory of the shot is to understand that the ball follows the angle the clubhead travels after impact. So, to hit a low shot, you should do things to keep the clubhead low after impact. To hit a high shot, you should do things to make the clubhead come up quickly after impact.

To hit the ball low, you should make three out-of-balance adjustments:

First, position the ball back in your stance and open your feet to the target line so your shoulders remain square. This places your hands in front of the ball, effectively delofting the clubface. This also makes the low point well in front of the ball, thereby ensuring that the clubhead stays low after impact.

Second, put most of your weight on your front foot. This places you farther in front of the ball and steepens your angle of attack into the ball, creating a lower trajectory.

Third, keep your wrists very firm into and past the impact area, resulting in a *very low finish.* Any premature flipping of the hands puts the loft back on the club, causing the ball to go too high.

Over Trouble

There are times when you want to hit the ball abnormally *high*. This might be when you have to go over a tree or when you are playing downwind. You make the same three out-of-balance adjustments as for a low shot, just in the opposite direction:

First, play the ball forward in your stance. If you have a good lie, you can move the ball to a position under the left armpit. (Any move farther forward may cause you to top or thin the ball.) This places the ball in a position where the clubhead will contact it just before the clubhead starts to rise.

Second, put most of your weight on your back foot. This positions you farther behind the ball and also shallows out your angle of approach.

Third, release your wrists fully so the club recocks quickly after impact. This will pull your hands into a high finish.

Note: To hit the driver lower and higher, merely adjust the height you tee the ball. Tee the ball lower for low shots, higher for high shots, then simply make your normal swing.

FOR A HIGH SHOT, POSITION THE BALL FORWARD IN YOUR STANCE . . .

Around Trouble

There are times when you have to curve the ball to go either around an obstacle or around a dogleg or into a tucked pin position.

CURVING RIGHT TO LEFT. To play a quick hook around trouble, make one simple adjustment. Align your body slightly to the right of where you want the ball to start, then before taking your grip, close the clubface to create the amount of hook you want. (This will require some experimentation and practice—there is no set formula for the amount to close the clubface.) Then make your normal swing. Remember that closing the face also makes the ball go lower with more roll, so allow for that.

To play a gentle hook (draw), rather than presetting the clubface you change the clubface alignment *during the swing* by rolling it closed with your

. . . AND FINISH HIGH TO SEND THE BALL HIGH OVER TROUBLE.

FOR A QUICK HOOK, AIM RIGHT
AND CLOSE THE CLUBFACE.

FOR A GENTLE DRAW, THINK OF
SPILLING WATER OVER YOUR LEFT
SHOULDER.

FOR A QUICK SLICE, AIM LEFT AND OPEN
THE CLUBFACE.

FOR A GENTLE FADE, THINK OF SPILLING
WATER OUT TO YOUR RIGHT.

PERFECTLY BALANCED GOLF

arms. So you align both your body and the clubface to the right of your target, then rotate your right arm over your left through the hitting area. Again, practice will tell you how much to roll. A good image is to think of spilling a bucket of water to your left after impact.

CURVING LEFT TO RIGHT. To play a slice around trouble, you follow the same procedure as for the quick hook, just in the opposite direction. First, align your body slightly to the left of where you want the ball to start, and then *before taking your grip,* open the clubface a sufficient amount to produce the curve you are looking for. Then take your normal swing. Once again, practice tells you how much to adjust your body alignment and clubface. *A note of caution:* When you open the face, the ball goes higher and shorter, so take plenty of club.

To play a gentle fade, rather than presetting the clubface rotate it open through the hitting area. Align both your body and the clubface to the left of your target, then rotate your right arm under your left arm through impact. Use the bucket image, but spill the water to your right after impact.

From Funny Lies

Here I will discuss (1) hitting from the rough, (2) hitting from tight or bare lies, (3) hitting from a fairway bunker, and (4) playing from slopes.

HITTING FROM THE ROUGH. In the rough, you can have three grades of lies: a good lie, where the ball is sitting on top of the grass; a medium lie, where the ball is sitting between the top of the grass and the ground; and a bad lie, where the ball is sitting deep in the grass.

When you are playing from a good lie, the danger is going underneath the ball, so a good image is to play the shot as you would a driver, since the ball is sitting on a "tee" of grass. Position the ball forward (under your left armpit) and sweep it off the top of the grass. The shot will tend to go higher than normal.

When you are playing from a medium lie, you will always get grass between the clubface and the ball. In all cases, this will reduce backspin and

BALL POSITION FROM THE ROUGH.

FROM A TIGHT
LIE, FINISH WITH
YOUR RIGHT
SHOULDER
HIGHER THAN
NORMAL.

*"I've found that
when that club
hits the ground, it
has a tendency to
square the face."*
—HARVEY PENICK

increase roll. If the rough is light, the ball will actually fly and roll farther than normal (called a "flyer"), and you will have to allow for this. If the grass is thick, the ball will fly shorter but roll farther. In playing this shot, simply use your normal ball position and swing, but preset the clubface slightly open because the grass tends to grab the hosel of the club, thereby closing the face through impact.

When you are playing from a bad lie, imagine that the ball will react as if you were hitting it with a headcover on the club. Your main goal should be to advance the ball as far as possible and get it back into play. To play the shot, set up with these out-of-balance adjustments: position the ball back in your stance, with the clubface open and your weight on your front foot. These adjustments will make your angle of attack steeper, thereby reducing the amount of grass that interferes with your swing. This setup angle of approach requires that you take plenty of loft in your club selection.

HITTING FROM TIGHT OR BARE LIES. These are situations where there is little air underneath the ball. It is sitting on bare or nearly bare dirt or sand. The key here is to hit the ball before hitting the ground. To do this, you should make the following out-of-balance adjustments: (1) play the ball back in your stance so you will hit it on the downswing, (2) keep your right shoulder high through the hitting area (dropping your right shoulder causes you to hit the shot fat), and (3) plan on the ball going lower than normal.

HITTING FROM A FAIRWAY BUNKER. Because of the distance involved in most fairway-bunker shots, your goal here is to hit the ball before hitting the sand, much like playing from a bare lie. In order to make similar out-of-balance adjustments: (1) dig your feet into the sand so you won't sink or

IN A FAIRWAY BUNKER, POSITION THE BALL SLIGHTLY BACK IN YOUR STANCE . . .

. . . CHOKE DOWN ON THE CLUB . . .

. . . AND FINISH WITH YOUR RIGHT SHOULDER HIGHER THAN NORMAL.

slip while swinging, (2) choke down on the club to, in effect, stiffen the shaft (this means you need to take one club more than you normally would for that distance), and (3) keep your right shoulder high through the hitting area.

When the shot calls for more distance from a fairway bunker, a good option is to use a lofted fairway wood rather than a long iron. The wider bottom on the fairway wood causes the club to slide through the sand rather than dig in. So when you are playing a lofted wood from a fairway bunker, follow these steps: (1) dig your feet in, (2) choke down on the club, (3) open the clubface slightly and align your body slightly to the left (this lowers the trailing edge of the club, giving it that sliding effect), and (4) position your hands even with the back of the ball and not in front of it. Positioning your hands in front causes the club to dig in.

Rules of the fairway bunker: (1) take enough loft to get out, (2) take enough club to get on, and (3) swing within yourself.

ON SIDE SLOPES, IMAGINE HOW THE BALL WOULD ROLL. IT WILL FLY IN THE SAME DIRECTION.

PLAYING FROM SLOPES. When the ground from which you are playing is not level, you must make out-of-balance adjustments. There are four such possibilities: (1) uphill lie, (2) downhill lie, (3) ball above your feet, and (4) ball below your feet.

The best way to recognize what the ball is prone to do from these different lies is to imagine what it would do if you rolled it along the ground. The ball will do the same thing in the air. For example, from an uphill lie, the ball would roll higher and shorter; from a downhill lie, it would roll lower and farther; with the ball above your feet, it would roll to your left; and with the ball below your feet, it would roll to your right.

Uphill lie. Once you know that the ball will go higher and shorter, your first adjustment is to take more club to reach your target. How much more club depends on how steep the slope is. When playing the shot, position your body so it parallels the slope, as opposed to leaning into the slope. When you adjust your position this way, your weight will go to your downhill foot. Rather than fighting gravity by trying to move up the slope as you swing, merely move the ball back in your stance to where you feel your weight is located. Then just go ahead and swing flat-footed and the ball will be located at the bottom of your swing arc.

Downhill lie. Once you know that the ball will go lower and farther, the first adjustment is to take a more lofted club than normal. Again, the severity of the slope determines the amount of loft you add to your club selection. When playing the shot, again adjust your position so your body parallels the slope. When you adjust to this position, your weight will go to your downhill foot. Once again, place the ball where you feel your weight is located. This will ensure you hit the ball at the bottom of the swing arc. Here's a tip to keep you from sliding your body down the slope as you

POSITION YOUR SHOULDERS PARALLEL WITH THE GROUND ON UPHILL SLOPES, THEN SWING ALONG THE SLOPE.

ON DOWNHILL SLOPES, BE SURE TO FINISH LOW TO THE GROUND.

swing: Square your left foot to the target line much as a skier does while going across a slope. As you swing, the worst mistake you can make is to try to lift the ball off the slope. Make sure you follow through *down* the slope, allowing the loft of the club to lift the ball up.

Ball above your feet. Once you know that the ball will go to the left, your first adjustment in playing this shot is to change your alignment to the right. There are two factors that make the ball go to the left. First, the loft of the club: the more loft, the more to the left the ball will go; the less loft, the less to the left the ball will go. Second, the steeper the slope, the more the loft will be pitched to the left. The only adjustment in playing this shot is in your aim

TIP: WHEN THE BALL IS ABOVE YOUR FEET, THE MORE LOFT, THE MORE LEFT.

and alignment. There is no need to choke down on the club. If the slope is so severe that balance is a problem, you may have to take more club and swing easier.

Ball below your feet. Once you know that the ball will go to the right, your first adjustment is to aim to the left. Practice will tell you how much. In playing this shot, there are two adjustments to make. First, sole the club flat on the ground behind the ball before you take your stance. Second, set up to this soled club by establishing your balance evenly on your feet. This will get the correct bend in both your knees and hips. If your weight is too much on the heels, you won't have enough hip bend; and if your weight is too much on your toes, you won't have enough knee bend.

Practicing trouble shots helps your whole game. If you know how to play from trouble, you won't be afraid of it and you will be more relaxed on your other shots. Then they will be more successful. Practicing these fundamentals also tells you how much adjustment to make from varying lies. So be sure to include trouble shots in your practice routine.

How to Balance
Your Emotions

A champion golfer has excellent skills with the body, the mind, and the heart. I've already talked about the physical techniques needed to become a balanced player. When I talk about the heart of a champion, I mean such things as focus, courage, poise under pressure, coping with success and adversity. I believe a sport psychologist should deal with these issues of emotion. But when I talk about the mental game, I'm really talking about strategy and tactics. (I am not trying to tread in an area that is best served by specialists in psychology. I am trying to use my expertise as a golf instructor to share with you the best ideas I have accumulated to help you score at your best level.)

Let's get our terminology straight. *Strategy* is really the plan you decide to use to best overcome the challenges of the situation. *Tactics* are the tools you use to best work your strategy. For instance, if you are playing a short, tight golf course, your strategy might be to keep the ball in play off the tee and attack the pins with your iron game. Your tactics to do this might include hitting less club off the tee, or maybe playing a shorter-flying fade for control and then concentrating on your short game so you can be bolder in going for the pins. So I am going to discuss how to have the best *balanced* strategy to play golf and will give you some specific tactics to achieve that strategy.

Several years ago I tested more than 1,200 golfers to try to determine how people of varying handicaps really do play golf. Golf is actually a game of four different situations: (1) tee shots (on par 4s and par 5s), (2) advancement shots (those shots that can't reach the green), (3) target shots (those that you expect to reach the green with), and (4) short-game shots. I tested golfers of all different abilities in each of those areas.

In the tee-shot area, I tried to determine the longest club people could hit in the fairway a reasonable number of times (50 percent of total shots for most groups). So I had the players each hit 20 shots from the tee with a driver, 3-wood, 5-wood, and the next-longest club they had.

After testing all of the players in driving, I tested them in the advancement-shot category to determine the longest club they could hit off the ground and keep the ball in the fairway a reasonable number of times. I had them hit twenty shots each with a 3-wood, a 5-wood, and the next-longest club they had.

Next, I tested them in the target-shot category. I wanted to find the *farthest* distance from the green a player could be and hit the green 50 percent of the time. So the women I started 50 yards from the green and had them hit twenty shots, the same from 75 yards, 100 yards, 125 yards, and 150 yards. The men I started at 75 yards and then had them move back in 25-yard increments.

I tested all of the short-game skills, including short putts, long putts, chips, pitches, and bunker play.

The results were eye-opening.

TEE-SHOTS. I found no one with a handicap higher than 14 who could hit a driver in play 50 percent of the time. So what that means is unless your handicap is 14 or under, you shouldn't use a driver! I found that no one with a handicap of 29 or higher could pass the test with either a driver or a 3-wood. What that means is if your handicap is higher than 29, you should tee off with a 5-wood or less club!

I wondered about the reason for these startling results and did some investigating. If your handicap is in the middle to high range, your ball flight is either short or crooked or both. The formula for distance is *mass × velocity*. Well, the lightest club in your bag is the driver. Next lightest is your 3-wood. So if you don't have enough clubhead speed, you need more clubhead weight. So for light hitters, your fairway woods will go farther than your driver. I found that unless you have 85 miles per hour of clubhead speed, your 3-wood will fly farther than your driver!

Also, a club with more loft will go straighter than a less-lofted club because a lot of sidespin is turned into backspin. So most people will hit the 3-wood or 5-wood longer and straighter than the driver.

ADVANCEMENT SHOTS. Here I discovered a similar breakdown. I found no one with a handicap of 15 or higher who could pass the test with a 3-wood. I found no one with a handicap of 28 or higher who could pass the test with a 3-wood or 5-wood. The same *mass × velocity* considerations apply, but there is another factor. Looking at the illustration below, you can see that on a perfectly struck 3-wood the club contacts the ball less than $1/8$ inch below its center. To get the ball in the air, you must hit below center. Therefore, there's not much room to make a mistake before you top the ball.

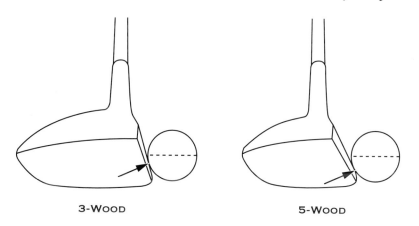

3-WOOD 5-WOOD

WHY IS A 5-WOOD A BETTER CHOICE FROM THE FAIRWAY THAN A 3-WOOD? BECAUSE THE HIGHER-LOFTED CLUB WILL CONTACT THE BALL MORE BELOW ITS EQUATOR, MAKING IT EASIER TO GET THE BALL AIRBORNE.

TARGET SHOTS. In the target-shot area, I found no one with a handicap of 8 or higher who could hit the green one-half the time from 150 yards. I found no one with a handicap of 15 or higher who could hit the green one-half the time from 125 yards. I found no one with a handicap of 30 or higher who could hit the green one-half the time from the minimum distances tested (75 yards for men and 50 yards for women).

SHORT-GAME SHOTS. The tests were similar, even though they didn't require distance. Good players are better than not-so-good players at all skills.

So this testing led me to the following tactics for differing handicap levels:

- Players with handicap levels of 36 and higher should tee off with no more than a 5-wood. After that, the longest club you should play from the ground would be a 5-iron. Until you are within 40 yards of the hole, you should play toward the safe part of the green. If you miss the green, use only your sand wedge for short shots and then use your putter on the green and from smooth fringes.

- Players with handicaps of 15 to 35 should use no more than a 3-wood from the tee, use nothing longer than a 5-wood from the ground, and always play toward the safe part of the green until they get inside 100 yards for men and for women with handicaps of 15 to 20, and inside 50 yards for women with handicaps of 21 and higher. You should use a low-running club for chips, and a sand wedge for high shots around the green.

- For tournament players, I would recommend the following tactics, which I devised for LPGA professional Shirley Furlong in 1984. She improved her scoring dramatically. She was a very conservative player and rarely shot at the pin. To counterbalance this tendency and make her more aggressive, I color-coded her clubs this way: 7-iron to putter = green; 5- and 6-iron = yellow; 4-iron through driver = red. If she had a green club, she shot at the pin no matter where it was; if she had a yellow club, she shot at the pin if the penalty was not a penalty stroke (water, out of bounds, unplayable lie); and if she had a red club, she was to play to the safest area.

So her round would go like this (for comparison with your game, she hit her 7-iron 150 yards): If she could drive the ball into a green-club zone, she would hit her tee shot toward a position to best shoot at the pin. If she couldn't, she would hit her tee shot toward the best position to reach a safe place on the green (see drawing). These tactics will make you a more balanced player. Aggressive players will have a time to be conservative (red clubs) and conservative players will have a time to be aggressive (green clubs). Since the formula is based on which club you use, the average distance you hit the ball won't matter.

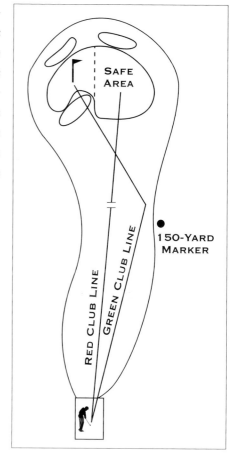

KNOWING WHEN TO USE YOUR RED CLUBS AND YOUR GREEN CLUBS CAN SAVE YOU STROKES DURING A ROUND.

TWELVE

Drills

It is helpful to remember that corrections may throw you off for a while.
If I knelt on my knees and played for a long time, it would throw me off
to swing while standing on my feet.

—HARVEY PENICK

"If I was going to
pick something
up, I'd put fingers
on both sides of
it."

—HARVEY PENICK

Two-Tees Drill Promotes Balanced Grip

Take two tees and place the narrow part of one between the thumb and forefinger of your left hand, then place the other between the thumb and forefinger of your right hand, so the wide parts of the tees extend upward. Then, keeping the tees in position, put your hands on the club using your normal grip. If the tees are pointing to the left of your face, your grip is too weak.

Turn your hands to the right on the club until the tees point toward your right eye. Close your eyes and feel how your hands are positioned on the club. Then with your eyes open and without the tees, practice putting your hands on the club in the same manner. This is a great drill to do when you're watching TV, to ingrain the feeling of a correct grip.

Tee-to-Retee Drill Teaches Earlier
Wrist Cock on Both Sides of Ball

Place a tee in the butt end of the grip of a middle iron and put two tees in the ground along the target line, one about 3 feet directly behind the ball, the other about 3 feet in front. Then take your normal setup and swing the club back, consciously cocking the club so the tee in the grip points to the tee behind the ball. Then on the through swing, purposefully uncock your wrists so the tee in the grip points to the tee in front of the ball. This drill will train your hands, arms, and wrists to uncock the clubhead earlier on the downswing, thereby helping to square the clubface at impact and counter-balancing a slice or low shot.

1.

2.

Wristwatch Drill Rotates Clubface

To practice rotating the clubface, hit some balls on the range while wearing a watch on your left wrist. On the backswing, feel as if the face of the watch remains faceup; on the follow-through, feel as if it faces down. This is an excellent way to train your left arm to rotate in a counterclockwise position through impact, thereby helping to square up the clubface and counterbalancing a slice.

1.

2.

Chip-Punch Drill Minimizes Wrist Rotation, Early Release, and High Ball Flight

Using a pitching wedge, preset your impact position, putting your hands forward until your left wrist is flat and your right wrist is bent. Then hit chip shots, keeping your wrists in the same position back and through. Next, repeat the drill using your 8-iron, swinging your arms back to 9 o'clock (parallel with the ground). Finally, hit a punch shot with the same motion, keeping your left wrist flat and your right wrist bent through impact. This drill will help keep the clubface from turning over through impact, create a later release for more distance, and produce a lower ball flight.

1.

2.

3.

Hula Hoop Drill Teaches Reverse-Roll Release

Take a Hula Hoop (can be purchased at any kids' store) and hold it with your normal golf grip. Pretend you are setting up to a ball and the Hula Hoop describes the plane and arc of your swing. This will automatically put your hands and wrists in a delayed wrist-cock position. Now, swing the Hula Hoop back and through as if it were a golf club rotating around your body. Try to keep the Hula Hoop on the plane of your swing. Notice that your body will turn back and through, but your hands will maintain the delayed wrist-cock position. That is the feeling of a reverse-roll release, which helps to counterbalance a hook.

1.

2.

3.

Two-Clubs Drill Aids Square Alignment

On the practice range, place a long iron on the ground along your target line. Align the club at a distant tree or target pin. Then place another long iron parallel to the first one, but along your stance line. Rehearse walking into your setup from down the line and practice looking at your target from this setup position. You *know* this position is square, so after a while you will be confident that you understand what a square alignment looks and feels like while you're set up over the ball. A square alignment is the first step to counterbalancing both pulls and pushes.

Left-Side-Against-Wall Drill Determines Correct Spine Tilt and Lowers Ball Flight

To understand the feeling of a correct spine tilt at address, find a wall—either indoors or out—and place your left side (hip, arm, and shoulder) against it. Pretend you are setting up to a ball, so your left side remains in contact with the wall, your right side forming a reverse K. This spine tilt promotes a swing path that comes into the ball from inside the target line, which will counterbalance pulled shots. At the range, try hitting shots with the left-side-against-wall image in your mind. This counterbalance will lower your ball flight.

Tilt-the-T Drill Establishes Correct Posture

If you have a problem pulling your shots, chances are your posture is too vertical. If you stand too upright with your chest and not enough with your legs, try the Tilt-the-T Drill: (1) stand tall to the ball, with your club perpendicular to your spine; (2) tilt the T to the ground without bending your knees; and (3) flex your knees without changing your spine angle. This drill will help you get into a more horizontal posture, promoting a swing path that counterbalances a pull.

1.

2.

3.

Three-Ball-Gate Drill Encourages Correct Hip Slide

If you are having trouble keeping your right elbow close to your side on the downswing, resulting in the classic "over the top" move, this drill may help. On the practice range, place a ball on the ground on your target line. Then place a second ball two inches behind it, just outside the target line. Finally, place a third ball 2 inches ahead of the first ball, just inside the target line. Now set up to the middle ball, with your body square to the target line. Try to hit the middle ball, the clubhead missing the other two balls. This may be difficult at first, but after a few shots, you will learn to swing so your arms deliver the club into the middle ball on an inside path, creating a solid hit, thus counterbalancing the out-to-in swing path that results in pulled shots.

1.

2.

Jump-Rope Drill Promotes Turn, Not Tilt

To understand the feeling of the body turning with a minimum of lateral movement, try this drill given to me by fellow professional Mike Dunaway. Hold a jump rope attached like a pulley to a fixed point (a clubshaft in the photos). First, pull the rope back with your right hand, arm, shoulder, and hip (the backswing), then pull the rope through with your left hand, arm, shoulder, and hip (the through swing). This is the feeling you want in a balanced swing, your body turning, not sliding back and through.

1.

2.

Headcover-Under-Right-Arm Drill Promotes Better Connection

If your right arm is separating too much from your body on the backswing, your arm swing becomes too upright, leading to an outside-in swing path and pulled shots. Try hitting practice balls with a headcover under your right armpit. This will keep your right arm connected to your body throughout your swing, thereby counterbalancing shots that start to the left.

Variable-Ball-Position Drill Straightens Swing Path

If you feel your downswing swing path is correct but your shots still tend to start to the left, your ball position could be the culprit. Try this counterbalance drill. With a club on the ground to indicate your target line, first hit practice shots with your normal ball position. Pay keen attention to where the ball starts in its flight. If it's starting left of your target line, position the next few balls well back in your stance, toward your right foot. This may cause you to hit severe pushes, because you are now contacting the ball while the club is coming from inside the target line. Gradually move your ball position forward until your shots start on line or slightly to the right of your target. That is your optimal ball position.

1.

2.

Right-Arm, Left-Arm Drill Ensures
Square Alignment

Square alignment is often an illusion. Many golfers think they line up their bodies (feet, hips, shoulders) directly at the target. But that only causes them to line up too far to the right. Actually, they need to line up *parallel left* of the target. To understand this, from directly behind the ball point your right forefinger directly at your target. Then extend your left arm out parallel with your right. Your left arm—not your right—indicates the line along which your body should follow at address.

Quarterback-Snap Drill Indicates Proper Posture

To understand how a balanced posture should feel, find a football and pretend you are a quarterback taking the snap from the center. Put your left hand above your right, so your right shoulder is slightly lower than your left. Your weight should be balanced on the balls of your feet, your legs slightly flexed, your spine relatively straight, and your arms poised to handle the snap. You are in an athletic position, ready to spring into action—the feeling you should have when you set up to hit a golf ball.

Tripod Drill Encourages Less Tilt in Your Setup

If you have too much tilt to the right in your setup position, your swing path likely will come into the ball too much from inside the target line, thereby starting shots too much to the right. To counterbalance this tendency, think of your legs and club as a tripod at address. This position effectively reduces the tilt in your spine (as seen from face-on), resulting in a swing path that comes into the ball from more along the target line, thus reducing the tendency to push the ball.

PERFECTLY BALANCED GOLF

Chair-by-Left-Leg Drill
Helps Clear Hips

If you tend to slide your hips into the ball rather than clear them to the left, your swing path will approach the ball too much from inside the target line, resulting in shots that start to the right. To counterbalance this hip slide, practice hitting shots—or just swinging a club at home—with a chair placed next to your left thigh. As you swing the club into the ball, focus on turning your hips to the left, missing the chair. If you slide your hips too much on the downswing, you'll know it because they will be blocked by the chair. Your shots will soon start more down the target line instead of out to the right.

Right-Side-to-Left-Foot Drill Promotes Leftward Path

To make sure your swing path goes along the target line, instead of out to the right, try this counterbalance drill. Set up to a ball on the practice range and stick the tip of your umbrella vertically into the ground opposite your left foot, a couple of inches outside the target line. Make your normal backswing, and on the through swing make sure your right side goes past the umbrella. This follow-through position ensures that you do not hang back with your body, which can cause an overly inside-out swing path and pushed shots.

Headcover-Under-Left-Arm Drill Encourages Left-Arm Connection

One cause of pushed shots is a tendency for the left arm to separate from the body on the follow-through. This is partly the result of many years of instruction in which golfers have been told to "finish high." To encourage the counterbalance of your left arm swinging back to the left after impact, hit practice balls with a headcover tucked under your left armpit. While this may seem awkward at first, it is a sure way to encourage your swing path to travel back to the left after impact, resulting in shots that start down the target line instead of out to the right.

Tees-Left-After-Impact Drill Establishes
Correct Ball Position

This drill will help you determine if your ball position needs to be farther forward in your stance, which would encourage you to swing the club back to the left after impact, thus counterbalancing a push. Place a ball on a tee in what you consider to be your normal ball position. Then place a second tee an inch forward of that ball and slightly left of the target line. Also place a third tee even farther forward and left of the second tee. Now hit the teed ball and take note of its starting line. Then put a ball on the second tee. Try to keep your feet in their original position and hit that ball. Finally, do the same for a ball on the third tee, the one farthest forward and left. What do the shots do in relation to each other? Repeat the drill a few times until you get a sense of how your ball position affects the starting flight of your shots. The farther forward you position the ball in your stance, the less will be your tendency to push your shots.

Address-Ball-off-Heel Drill
Prevents Toed Shots

If your problem is hitting too many shots on the toe of the club, an obvious solution is to stand closer to the ball. But standing closer is not always as easy as it sounds. It may feel awkward to you. This drill will help. Hit practice shots addressing the ball off the heel of the club. This counterbalance will serve to improve your backswing and downswing paths, thereby encouraging you to deliver the clubhead into the ball more solidly. Some players—Fuzzy Zoeller is one example—actually address the ball off the heel while playing shots on the course, so don't be afraid to try it.

Half-Swing Drill Helps Maintain Posture

If you suspect you come out of your posture during your swing, which can cause toe hits, try this counterbalance drill. On the range, set up with a 5-iron in your normal, correct posture. Then swing the club halfway back and hold that position. Your spine angle should be the same as it was at address. Now swing through to a half-finish position. Again, your spine angle should be the same as at address. Hit several balls from a tee with these half-swings while concentrating on holding your posture constant throughout.

1.

2.

Tee-in-Front-of-Ball Drill Promotes
Left-Arm Extension

If hitting shots on the toe is plaguing your game, you may not be extending your left arm through impact. Try hitting practice shots, placing a tee an inch in front of the ball on the target line before you take your setup. After impact, strive to make the clubhead strike the tee. This counterbalance will greatly enhance your left-arm extension through the ball, thereby promoting more solid contact.

"When that left leg straightens too early, you'll have a tendency to come across the ball; keeping that knee flexed a little bit lets that club go down the line."
—HARVEY PENICK

Dollar-Bill-Divots Drill Reduces
Clubface Rotation

If your clubface is rotating excessively open on the backswing and closed on the through swing, try to make divots that look like dollar bills. Examine your divots on the practice tee. Are they thin or narrow? Are they inconsistent? Are they wide at the front and narrow at the back? Are they deep on one side and shallow on the other? If so, this drill is for you. First, without a ball, make a series of divots along an imaginary line indicating your ball position. Ideally, your divots should start just targetward of that line and be about the length and width of a dollar bill. To achieve such divots, you may need to feel yourself actually closing the clubface on the backswing and opening it on the through swing. This action will help keep the clubface square to the target line longer. You can actually check your divots by placing a real greenback inside them. When you can consistently make dollar-bill-sized divots without a ball, try hitting balls on the range while focusing on making those same types of divots.

PERFECTLY BALANCED GOLF

Address-Ball-off-Toe Drill Stops Heeled Shots

Just as the most basic counterbalance for toed shots is to play the ball off the heel of the club, the most basic counterbalance for heeled shots is to play the ball off the toe of the club. This address counterbalance forces you to stand a bit farther from the ball, promoting a swing path back and through that results in fewer heeled shots and more solid contact.

Cigar Drill Maintains Posture

I don't generally advocate smoking cigars, but this is a good drill for keeping your posture steady throughout the shot, thus counterbalancing shots hit on the heel. Place a ball on a tee and place another tee a couple of inches to the right of the ball as you look at it from your address position and slightly outside the target line. Now set up to the ball with a cigar in your mouth. Aim the cigar at the tee that is to the right of the ball. As you swing, keep the cigar pointed at the tee. This drill will encourage you to keep your head from bobbing up or down, thus helping you maintain your posture through impact. As a result, you will soon be hitting the ball more in the center of the club. (If you don't want to use a cigar, use a ballpoint pen.)

Take-a-Bow
Drill Maintains Radius

To make sure your arms don't extend farther at impact than they were set at address, thereby causing heeled or fat shots, try the Take-a-Bow Drill. Stand to the ball with your feet your normal stance-width apart, your back vertical, and the club extended directly in front of you. Use your normal grip to hold the club. Now simply bend over from the waist, flexing your knees slightly. This counterbalance procedure premeasures the distance you should be standing from the ball, assuming your arms are fully extended at impact, as they should be. This procedure should feel as if you were giving someone a bow of respect.

One-Third-Back-and-Square-Through Drill
Eliminates Clubface Rotation

If your clubface is rotating excessively back and through, causing you to hit shots on the heel, or even to shank the ball, try this drill. Start by hitting short shots with a pitching wedge. Take your normal setup and swing the club one-third of the way back. Strive to have the clubface looking at the ball at this point. Then on the follow-through, strive to have the clubface square to the target line. Little by little proceed to longer clubs, but continue swinging back only to one-third, so you can see and feel if the clubface is looking at the ball on the backswing. This counterbalance should greatly reduce your clubface rotation and encourage contact with the ball in the center of the clubface.

"When that left leg straightens too early, you'll have a tendency to come across the ball; keeping that knee flexed a little bit lets that club go down the line."

—HARVEY PENICK

1.

2.

PERFECTLY BALANCED GOLF

Doorjamb Drill Maintains Correct Posture

This drill will help you maintain your posture through impact, instead of allowing your body to pull up, which results in thin or topped shots. Practice making swings while placing your head against a doorjamb in an open doorway. Rehearse turning back and through while getting the feeling of making your spine retain a consistent angle, the angle you established at address. When you hit balls on the range, keep this image in mind as a counterbalance to topped or thin shots.

Hitting-Balls-from-a-Line Drill Establishes Ball Position

To determine the ball position that is correct for your swing, first make a line in the turf of your practice range. Borrow a can of spray paint from your pro or course superintendent or merely scratch a line in the grass with a tee or club perpendicular to your target line. Then set up to the line so it indicates your ball position—say, off your left heel. Now make practice swings, noting where your divots occur in relation to the line. Adjust your ball position accordingly until you know exactly where it should be. (The divots in the accompanying photo indicate that the ball position should be moved back in the stance.)

Feet-Together Drill Reduces Lateral Movement

If you have too much lateral movement in your swing, it is difficult to hit the ball solidly. You are likely to hit the ball either fat or thin. Try the counterbalance of hitting balls on the practice range with your feet together, even touching. Start with a middle or short iron, the ball on a tee. You will soon feel your arms and club rotating around your spine, not sliding from side to side. Eventually, alternate between shots with your feet together and shots with your normal stance width. When your feet are a normal width apart, focus on turning your torso rather than sliding back and forth, just as when your feet were together.

Hand-on-Forehead Drill Helps Maintain Posture

For this drill you need a partner. On the practice ground, set up to a teed ball with a middle iron. Take your normal, correct posture. Then before you hit, have a friend, standing outside the target line beyond the ball, lean over, extend his arm, and gently place his hand on your forehead. This may feel a bit disconcerting to you at first, but you will get used to it. Now go ahead and swing, hitting the ball down the range. You will know immediately if your head lowers (or rises) significantly during your swing. After impact, it's okay for your head to rise. And it's okay for your head to move a bit laterally. But it should maintain its general level position on the backswing and through impact. Now do the same for your friend.

Clubs-on-Ground Drill Improves Ball Position

If you are hitting shots too low, your ball position could be too far back in your stance. If your shots are too high, your ball position could be too far forward. To systematically and precisely check your ball position, lay three clubs on the ground on the practice tee. Place the first two clubs parallel to each other, one along the target line, the other along your stance line. Place the third club perpendicular to the two other clubs, to indicate ball position. Your ball position for most clubs and shots should be 1 inch left of the center of your stance. This should be opposite a point between the left side of your face and your left armpit. For safety, make sure the clubs are at least a clubhead length from the ball.

Uphill-Lie Drill Promotes Weight Back

If you suspect you need to place more of your weight on your back foot to help hit the ball higher, this drill might help. Find a slope near the practice range and position your body so you are faced with an uphill shot. Actually set up to a ball. Now ask yourself where most of your weight is placed. Toward your back foot, right? That's the feeling you may need on all of your shots from flat lies. Try hitting shots on the range with that same weight-back distribution. With this counterbalance you may find it easier to get the ball up in the air.

Shadow Drill Helps You Turn
Back and Through

You need an at least partially sunny day to perform this drill, but it will help you get behind the ball on the backswing and past the ball on the through swing. First, determine where the sun is located in the sky and put yourself in your normal address position so the sun directly hits your back, casting your shadow in front of you. Now place a club on the ground vertically along the top of your spine in your shadow. Next, swing another club back and through. On the backswing, check that your shadow is to the right of the club on the ground. On the follow-through, check that your shadow is to the left of the club on the ground. These two moves indicate that you have shifted your weight correctly on the backswing and again on the through swing.

"Turning is easy. Just pretend you're going to turn and say 'Hi, Doc' to the fellow next to you."
—HARVEY PENICK

Knockdown-Under-Rope Drill Promotes Later Release

If your shots are going too high, chances are you are releasing the club too early on the downswing. Here's a counterbalance drill to instill a later release in your swing. First, tie a rope between two objects, so it hovers parallel to the ground about 2 feet high. Next, from several feet away, take a short iron—an 8-iron, for instance—and practice hitting knockdown shots underneath the rope. Do whatever you feel is necessary to keep the ball low. You will find that the more you delay your release on the downswing and the more you limit your follow-through, the lower the ball will go. Keep practicing until you can hit the ball under the rope consistently.

"If I knew what caused that [casting the club], I'd be a rich man."
—HARVEY PENICK

Club-Across-Shoulders Drill Promotes Full Turn

To get the feeling of making a correct and full shoulder turn, hold a club across the front of your shoulders, along your collarbone. Your arms will be folded as you hold the club. Set up as if you were addressing a ball, so the club across your shoulders is parallel to the ground. Now turn back to your right as if you were swinging a golf club. Ideally, your left shoulder should be positioned over your right foot. This is how you should feel at the top of your swing, a powerful position from which you can deliver the club forcefully into the ball.

Weighted-Club Drill Increases Arm Swing

An excellent way to increase your swing arc is by becoming more flexible with your arms. Swinging a weighted club—something you can do inside during the colder months—is a fine method for achieving this flexibility because it also strengthens your golf muscles (hands, arms, wrists, shoulders). You can buy a weighted club or make one yourself. Simply purchase some lead tape at the hardware store and wrap several layers around the head of an old driver. Be sure to wrap a layer or two around the shaft of the club so you add weight to the overall club, not just the head. Then practice making normal swings *without a ball,* often stopping at the top of your swing, holding that position. Do this a few minutes every day and you'll be amazed how strong your swing is with your regular clubs.

"He had a little 'cowtail' move [downcock] up there."
—HARVEY PENICK

Preset Drill Increases Wrist Cock

The more you can cock your wrists, the more distance you can achieve. To learn to increase your wrist cock, try the Preset Drill. With, say, a 5-iron, set up in your normal address position. Without swinging your arms or moving your body, cock your wrists so the clubshaft is at least parallel to the ground. Check that position. Then swing your arms up and turn your shoulders. That should put you in a powerful position at the top of your swing. You will soon have the feeling of a tremendous amount of stored energy at the top of your swing, ready to be released into the ball. Do the drill a few times without a ball, then set up to a ball on the practice tee. Go through the same procedure, but don't stop at the top of the swing. Go ahead and hit the ball.

Three-90-Degrees Drill Ensures
Correct Top of Swing

This drill should be done in front of a full-length mirror, or use the reflection of a window. At the top of a balanced and powerful swing with a 5-iron, there are three 90-degree positions: (1) your wrist cock—the angle between the clubshaft and your left arm, (2) the angle of your right elbow, and (3) the angle of your shoulder turn. Set up with a 5-iron in front of your reflection and swing to the top. First, check your wrist cock. Is it 90 degrees? You should be able to draw a right angle on the mirror directly over your arm and clubshaft. If you can't, adjust your wrist cock and close your eyes until you know what 90 degrees feels like. Second, do the same with your shoulder turn. Your shoulders should have turned 90 degrees from their position at address. Finally, turn around so when you swing to the top, you must look over your right shoulder at your reflection. Note the angle of your right elbow. If it's not 90 degrees, adjust it and close your eyes until you know what it feels like. Repeat this drill until you consistently achieve 90 degrees in those three positions.

Swish Drill Increases Clubhead Speed

One of the most important ingredients of a swing that produces distance is high clubhead speed. To increase your RPMs, hold your driver or 3-wood at the hosel near the clubhead. Set up to an imaginary ball and swing the club so the handle end makes a swish sound. Try to make the swish as loud as possible, and make the noise the loudest at the bottom of the swing, where impact would be. Do this drill a few times every day and you will soon notice that your swing is free and unrestricted, your clubhead speed greatly increased.

Variable-Backswing Drill Promotes
Short-Game Distance Control

If you find that you have trouble predicting the distances your pitch shots travel, here is a drill that will help you. With your wedge on the practice tee, find a target your normal full-wedge distance away and hit a few shots to it with your normal full-swing backswing. Note how far they are traveling. Then shorten your backswing to three-quarters for a few shots. What happens? Now shorten your backswing so your left arm is at 9 o'clock (parallel with the ground). What happens? Of course those shots don't go as far, assuming solid contact. When you practice your short game, always remember to practice hitting pitches different distances with the same club. But control those distances with the *length* of your backswing, not the speed of your swing.

FIRST SWING.

SECOND SWING.

THIRD SWING.

PERFECTLY BALANCED GOLF

Firm-It-Up Drill Controls Full-Swing Distances

There are three "gears" in a golf swing. Controlling them is how you control the distance your shots travel. The three gears are shoulder turn, arm swing, and wrist cock. The surest way to reduce distance is by shortening either your turn, your arm swing, or your wrist cock. Practice hitting shots where you reduce one of the three gears. In other words, put your swing in second gear. For maximum control, limit your wrist cock. On the range, hit balls by swinging back and through and feeling as if you are hardly cocking your wrists at all. (You will probably still be cocking them more than you think.) This kind of distance control will improve your scores dramatically.

1-Inch, 2-Inch, 3-Inch Drill Encourages Earlier Release

From a fluffy lie on the practice ground, put a tee 1 inch behind the ball, directly on the target line. Then from the top of the backswing, try to release the club early enough to take the tee and the ball. Then do the same thing, but place the tee 2 inches, then 3 inches behind the ball. (The farther back you place the tee, the slightly more to the inside of the target line you must position it.) Soon your release will be early rather than late, thereby decreasing your distance but increasing your control.

Full-Swing, Variable-Distance Drill
Enhances Control

On the practice tee, place three balls along a line opposite your normal ball position for a 5-iron. First, hit the ball closest to you, making a full swing with your 5-iron. But try to make the ball travel *only one-third* the distance of your normal 5-iron. Next, hit the second ball, again with a full swing, but make it travel *only two-thirds* your normal 5-iron distance. Finally, hit the last ball the *full* 5-iron distance. Repeat the drill a few times until you learn how hard you need to swing to make the ball go different distances.

Plane-Board Drill Gets Putter
on Correct Path

On the practice green, find a relatively flat 8- to 10-foot putt. Take a piece of wood such as a sheet of plywood and prop it up with a pair of shafts on the line of the putt, so this plane board's angle matches the shaft angle of your putter when your putter is soled flat on the ground. Now practice stroking putts to the hole, keeping your putter's shaft lightly touching the plane board. If your putter's shaft stays true to its angle back and through, the blade, if square at address, will remain square *to its path* throughout the stroke. And it will be square at impact, which is the ultimate goal for making putts. This drill assures that the path of your putting stroke is balanced, swinging neither too much from the inside nor too much from the outside. Also with this drill, you don't have to worry about trying to keep the blade square to the target back and through. It will be looking at the target at impact without any manipulation on your part.

"I'd rather see a player hit a putt on the toe than on the heel."
—HARVEY PENICK

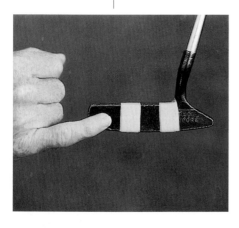

Band-Aid Drill Encourages Contact on Putter's Sweet Spot

To learn to hit your putts directly on the sweet spot of your putter, wrap two Band-Aids around the blade of your putter, framing the sweet spot. Make sure there is enough room between the Band-Aids for the ball to contact the putter blade. Now take your putter to the practice green and stroke some putts, starting with shorter ones. You will know quickly if you are striking the ball toward either the toe or the heel of the putter. The ball will come off the putter face "dead" as a result of hitting one of the Band-Aids. Practice until you can make contact with the sweet spot of your putter every time. You will notice that the ball will start rolling more consistent distances and that your putter face will stop twisting at impact. Unfortunately, you are not allowed to use the Band-Aids when you play, only in practice.

"Putt on the last hole just like you do on the first hole."

—HARVEY PENICK

Tee-to-Tee Drill Teaches Smooth Stroke

This drill will help you balance out your putting stroke if you are either decelerating or overaccelerating on the follow-through. Both faults result in off-line putts and inconsistent distance control, especially under pressure. Ideally, you want a stroke that is smooth throughout. That smoothness encourages your putter face to stay square to its line, thus promoting on-line putts. A smooth stroke comes from taking the putter back the same distance you follow through. On the practice green, find a relatively flat putt of medium distance. Place a tee in the ground at a point representing where you think your backswing should end. Place another tee equidistant to that point from the ball representing where your follow-through should end. Practice making that medium-length putt, the head of your putter swinging back and through to the tees. Notice that to do so encourages a smooth stroke. A constant grip pressure also makes it easier to take the putter back and through the same distance. Practice the same technique on putts of other distances until a balanced stroke back and through is your norm.

Closed-Eyes Drill Teaches Feel for Distance

If you are having trouble gaining the feel for longer putts, causing you to three-putt often, try this drill. On the practice green, pick a hole some 30 feet away. Then set up to the first of three balls you have placed on the putting surface. Before you stroke it, close your eyes. Then go ahead and hit the putt, trying to leave it a foot or so short of the hole. Without looking at the result, try to *feel* if you were successful. Do the same for the second ball, but focus on hitting it a couple of feet past the hole. Again, assess the result with your eyes still closed. Finally, try to make the third ball go exactly the right distance, also with your eyes closed. Repeat this drill often and your feel for distance will improve dramatically.

Roll-Ball-off-Ramp Drill Relates Backswing Length to Distance

The key to good distance putting is to understand that the longer the putt, the longer your swing should be. In other words, you should take the putter back and through farther instead of swinging it faster. To illustrate this, make a ramp by placing two clubs parallel to each other, $^3/_4$ inch apart. With the grip ends resting on the putting surface, raise the clubhead ends off the ground 1 foot. Then roll a ball down the ramp and onto the green, like a makeshift Stimpmeter (used to measure green speed). Notice how the higher up the shaft you start the ball rolling, the farther it will roll on the green. Think of the distance you take the putter back equating to the height you need to raise the ball to roll it the correct distance.

Under-Shaft Drill Promotes Low Backswing

If your putts are skidding or bouncing immediately after impact instead of rolling smoothly, chances are you're picking the putter up abruptly on the backswing, resulting in a glancing blow on the through swing. To counterbalance this tendency, try this drill on the practice green. First, find a putt of, say, 10 feet. Stick a shaft into the ground on an angle, so the grip end of the shaft hovers 2 inches above the path of your backswing. Now stroke a few putts, keeping the putter head under the shaft. Soon you will be taking the putter back low to the ground with your hands ahead of the putter head, resulting in a smoother-rolling ball.

"Don't forget how to putt when you start hitting it like that."
—HARVEY PENICK

2-Feet-Past Drill Encourages Aggressive Stroke

If you notice you come up short on your medium-length putts, practice hitting them 2 feet past the hole. How? Pretend the hole is 2 feet behind the real hole and mark that spot with a tee. Now try to roll the ball to the tee, letting the hole get in the way. Notice how many putts actually fall into the hole, even though the ball's speed is a little too fast. On the course, visualize a tee in the green 2 feet past the real cup and putt for the tee, not for the hole.

Tee-Around-Hole Drill Creates
Correct Putting Imagery

Find a putt on your practice green that has a consistent slope. Then start practicing an uphill putt of about 6 feet. Place a tee in the back of the cup and try to drive that tee deeper into the ground when putting uphill. This makes you mentally more aggressive. Then go to the opposite side of the hole, where you would be putting downhill. Place a tee in the back of the cup and try to make putts without hitting the tee. This encourages "feeding" the ball into the hole on downhill putts. Next, move to the right-to-left putt from the side of the hole and place a tee right in front of the cup. Then try to make putts missing the tee on the high side of the hole. This gives you the correct image for making breaking putts. Then do the same thing on the opposite side of the hole for left-to-right putts.

1.

3.

2.

4.

Bag-Holder Drill Teaches Pitching Trajectories

To learn how to vary the height of your short pitches, try this drill. Take a typical bag holder you'd find on a practice range and position yourself about 8 to 10 feet behind it. Then with your sand wedge, hit short pitch shots, trying to send the ball either under the top rung of the bag holder or over it. For the lower pitches, you must learn to position the ball back in your stance, with your weight and hands leaning toward the target. Minimize your follow-through, finishing with the clubhead low to the ground. For higher pitches, make sure you have a good lie. Position the ball more forward in your stance, your hands even with the ball, your weight evenly distributed. Make a fuller follow-through. This drill teaches you to experiment with your setup and technique until you can regulate the trajectory of your pitches.

Paint-a-Face-on-the-Face Drill
Encourages Technique for High Pitches

To learn the proper method for hitting high, soft pitches, take your sand wedge and actually paint or draw a cartoon face on the face of the club. Put two eyes, a nose, and a smile on it. Now hit practice shots. On the backswing, the cartoon face should be smiling at you. At impact, the face should still be smiling at you. And past impact, it should be smiling at you from an upside-down position. From time to time, make practice swings without a ball, holding the backswing and the follow-through steady to make sure the cartoon face is looking in the correct direction.

1.   2.   3.

Tee-in-the-Bunker Drill Teaches Proper Cut of Sand

The basic bunker technique is difficult for many golfers—beginners as well as experienced players—to understand because this is the only shot in the game in which you actually don't want to contact the ball with the club. You want the club to cut under the ball, taking a slice of sand with the ball. In the practice bunker, place the ball on a tee, the ball level with the top edge of the sand. When you swing, let the sand wedge clip the tee out from under the ball. This drill will encourage you to allow the flange of the sand wedge to take a shallow cut of sand from under the ball, sending the ball out of the bunker and onto the green. (The tee should fly out of the bunker and toward the hole as well.)

Sand-the-Flange Drill Promotes
Proper Sand Displacement

This is a nifty drill that is nearly guaranteed to balance out your sand technique, whether you're taking too much sand, thereby leaving the ball in the bunker, or taking too little sand, thereby thinning the ball over the green. It teaches you to use the flange of your sand wedge correctly. First, find a two-by-four board and paint it with a bright color (red or yellow is good). Next, after the paint dries, bury the board in a practice bunker so the top of the board is even with the top of the sand. Now, cover the board with ¼ inch of sand and place a ball on the sand. Try to hit the board with the skidding edge of your sand wedge, sending the ball out of the bunker and in effect "painting" the flange. (You should see paint from the board on the trailing edge of the flange.) Finally, place a ball in the sand away from the board and try to "sand" the paint off the flange as you extricate the ball from the sand. You can repeat this drill as many times as you want, keeping the sequence the same.

1.

2.

3.

4.

Afterword

This concept of balance—as well as the structure for this book—has been an idea of mine for quite some time. As my friend Ben Doyle says, it has been incubating. I've felt for a long time that golf should be taught in a more individualized way. As I've continued to watch the evolution of golf instruction and how golfers play, I've found more and more reason to believe this.

For years, golf was taught in America by professionals who either were from Scotland or were trained by professionals from Scotland. Consequently, there was a universally accepted way of teaching, with little dissension. With the advent of new equipment and the changes in golf course preparation, the norm began to change to accommodate these differing conditions. What would have been considered in balance eighty years ago would be out of balance today.

In the era of wooden shafts and unwatered fairways, the preferred ball flight was a sweeping draw to create roll and produce distance. The high twisting of the wooden shafts required a well-trained set of hands to coordinate this twisting clubhead into a reasonably square clubface. This facet required the swing to be relatively flat. Byron Nelson is credited with popularizing the "modern swing." The reason is that he was the first player to play well using what was considered an unorthodox swing. His more upright swing and reduced hand action created a higher ball flight, which fit the more groomed and less rolling fairways and the reduced amount of torque in the steel shafts that were just coming into vogue. In other words, his style of play was perfectly in balance for him and his time.

Jack Nicklaus was the next precursor of swing changes. His swing was even more upright than Nelson's, but his tremendous success made his style the most copied ever. During this time, the first real swing system, or "method," was promoted. The "square-to-square" system being authored by Dick Aultman and taught by such respected professionals as Jim Flick and Bill Strausbaugh became the rage, as it mimicked Nicklaus's swing. This period really created an interest in golf instruction. As it became financially more viable to make strictly teaching golf your profession, a number of people made that choice. While prior to this time the most noted teachers were those who were the best players, after this time the most noted teachers were those who began to do a lot of research into the science of playing and teaching golf. I was a member of this group, and I like to call us "yuppie" pros.

Among that group were Peter Kostis, Hank Haney, David Leadbetter, Rick Smith, Gary Wiren, Ben Doyle, and most of the other name teachers of this era. While there were still great players teaching great golf, such as Bob Toski and Paul Runyan, most of the gain in instruction was achieved by the "yuppie" pros.

This brought about the increased use of video, biomechanics, psychology, club fitting, and physical fitness in order to make the students the best they could be. Such an assault on the theories of playing and teaching golf brought both good and bad to the game. The bad, I feel, was that the "art" of golf took a back seat to the "science" of golf. However, the art is returning, thanks to the input of sport psychologists, who have helped balance out the emphasis on golf-swing mechanics with the use of those mechanics to produce great shotmaking.

The good, though, far outweighed the bad. A lot of old wives' tales about what's right and wrong in the golf swing were eliminated or placed in proper perspective, and finally a true understanding of cause and effect has been brought about. For a while, there was a continued effort to prove there was a "best" way to play or swing, and even today different camps profess their style as the only way to "do it right." There has been too much evidence, however, that there are a number of ways to play golf successfully, and the trend is to match up fundamentals and use each player's strengths to his or her best advantage.

There will always be the tendency to try to copy the players who are having the most success, but I don't see anyone trying to copy Tom Lehman's swing, or even Tiger Woods's swing. However, I do see players trying to copy Tiger's attitude about winning, as well as Lehman's work ethic. Players are finally realizing that what is good for someone else might not be good for them. They don't want to get out of balance.

Now that you have started to put your golf game in balance, the key is to find ways to keep it there. When you discover yourself emphasizing one part of your swing or another, or playing too aggressively or too conservatively, stop for a minute and assess what you are doing. I hope that with the skills you have learned from this book you will be able to stay balanced on and off the course, and that your game and your life will continually improve.

What I have tried to do in this book is provide a roadmap for you to match up your fundamentals so you can find *your* best game. While it is not easy to learn a complex motor skill from a book, it is important to have a guide. I hope I have provided you with that guide. There is a lot of knowledge from a lot of people in this book. In truth, there is not a lot of original material. But the physics and geometry of golf don't change. I hope the people who have shared their knowledge with me and recognize their words and thoughts here will take pride in knowing that my respect for them helped me try to help you. Enjoy!